# E-mail

## to the Front

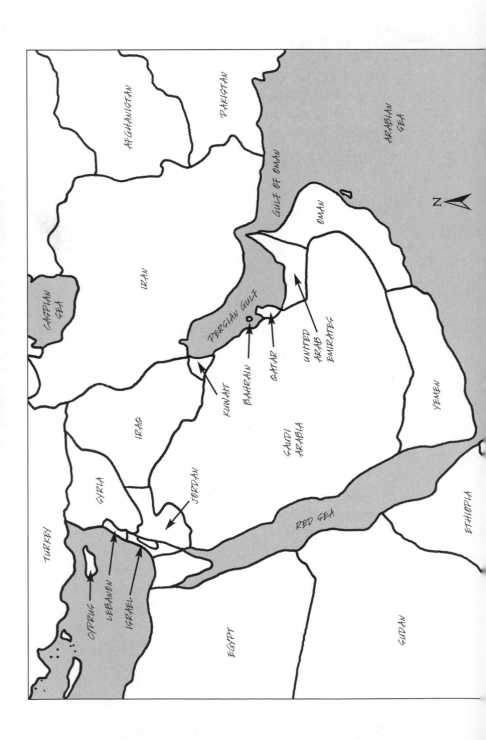

# E-mail
## to the Front

*One Wife's Correspondence with Her Husband Overseas*

Alesia Holliday

**Andrews McMeel
Publishing**

Kansas City

03 04 05 06 07 FFG 10 9 8 7 6 5 4 3 2 1

Library of Congress Cataloging-in-Publication Data

Holliday, Alesia.
   E-mail to the front : one wife's correspondence with her husband overseas /
   Alesia Holliday.
      p. cm.
   ISBN 0-7407-3575-6
      1. Holliday, Alesia—Correspondence. 2. Navy spouses—United States—
      Correspondence.
   3. McLevey, Judd—Correspondence. 4. United States. Navy—Flight officers—
      Correspondence. I. Title.

V62.H65 2003
359'.0092'2—dc21
[B]
                                                                2002043798

Composition by Steve Brooker at Just Your *Type*

---

**ATTENTION: SCHOOLS AND BUSINESSES**

To Judd, my personal hero:
*You believed in me even when I didn't. I love you more.*

To Connor, who loves me bigger than Earth:
*I love you bigger than Jupiter.*

To Lauren:
*May you always feel like a princess. I love you so much.*

To Mom, my number one fan:
*I'm yours, too. Cancer never had a chance.*

And, especially, to all Military Spouses everywhere:
*Thank you.*

# Contents

## Contents

# Contents

# Acknowledgments

This book, like everything that is best in life, would never have happened without the support of so many people:

Thanks to my wonderful editor, Kelly Gilbert, who loved my book even before anybody famous did. Your wisdom and insights made the book better in our first five-minute telephone conversation, and it has only gone uphill from there.

Thanks to Kristine Abbott and the entire Andrews McMeel team, for sharing my vision and excitement.

Thanks to Beverly Brandt, who read every word in every chapter and gave me tough feedback when I needed it and smiley faces when I didn't. Your grace, courage, and friendship have meant so much to me.

Thanks to Pam Binder, who loved the idea and convinced me I could do it. Your kindness and generosity of spirit helped me more than you know.

Thanks to Diane Hall-Harris, kind friend and great cheerleader. May 2003 be your year.

Thanks to Dave Barry, for taking the time to read something from a hopeful, unknown writer and for writing me back. It was the first time anything you wrote ever made me cry.

Thanks to Suzanne Brockmann, whose generosity is matched only by her talent and enthusiasm. May you always be as successful as you are kind.

Thanks to Bernie and Carrie Ryan, who offered friendship and support during Judd's deployment and during the writing of this book. Your ideas for the top ten list made me realize how universal our experiences really are.

Thanks to Clyde and Robin Porter, for their friendship and grace; and to Dan and Megan McNamera, for their kindness and support. All of you are wonderful examples of leadership in action.

And, of course, I never would have made it through deployment without the support of my family and friends:

Thanks—forever and always—to Lauren, Connor, and Judd. Every day you show me what is most important in life.

Thanks to my intrepid mother, venturing boldly out of tiny Barnesville to trek across the country and take part in our adventures. I hope to always have your courage, Mom.

Thanks to my terrific brother Jerry, whose sense of humor and quiet wisdom sustained me through some of the darkest days. You're the best!

Thanks to my brother Josh—may 2003 be better.

Thanks to Tricia and Dale Keller, for inviting us out to dinner to escape deployment for a little while.

Thanks to my friends: Mary True, who helped me see the ridiculous and told me she admired me when I so needed to hear it; and Malia Starmer, who was going through the same things at the same times; you both listened to me vent and helped me laugh.

Thanks to Lori Gellerson, the world's best neighbor; Bethany Stowell, who played and painted and cuddled with the kids so I could have a mental health break; my great friends at work, Carin Marney and Jodi Freudenberger, who understood, even though they didn't have children yet (*now* you get it!); Jan Stowell, for her kindness and support; and to Jeff Johnson and Doug Hofmann, who always brought a sense of humor to work with them.

Finally, a *huge* thank-you to my agent, Michelle Grajkowski, who loved this book so much she called her Grandma. Your talent and dedication are inspiring. Thank you for your excitement and enthusiasm (AACKK!), for phone calls at 1 A.M., and for helping me make my dreams come true. You are truly a blessing in my life.

# Introduction

**To:** My Readers
**From:** Alesia
**Subject:** Welcome to the world of military families!

You'd think I would have known better. I grew up as an Air Force brat—thirteen different schools by the time I graduated from high school. My mom used to say we should strap roller skates on the bottom of the couch, to make moving easier.

But then I met Judd and common sense flew out the window, as it tends to do when love gets involved. Before I knew it, I was saying yes to a wonderful man and life in the U.S. Navy.

Seven years, three states, and two children later, I can honestly say it's never been dull!

I first thought of writing *E-mail* when Judd was on deployment post-September 11, 2001. His squadron had been slated for a routine deployment to Japan, but the terrorist attacks on New York and DC changed everything. I knew he and his crew were flying missions over Afghanistan, and I was scared. One day, I found a computer file I had created after his previous deployment to the Middle East. It contained copies of all the e-mails we had sent back and forth during the long six months of absence. Reading back over them, I was surprised at how funny and poignant some of them were.

Like so many others, I was taking stock of my life in light of the tragedy our country had just endured. My children were happy and healthy; I had a good job, good friends, and a close family. All in all, I felt pretty lucky. But I hadn't done anything that would contribute to society on a large scale. Suddenly, that seemed very important to me. These circumstances came together in my mind over a period of several weeks and the idea for *E-mail* formed. It would be a book that could answer the questions everyone at work and all my nonmilitary friends asked: How do you *do* it? Move across the country with two young children, only to have your husband leave you for six months? Not know where he is, or if he's safe?

At the same time, I wanted the book to share a message of caring and hope with military spouses everywhere and with everyone who has ever juggled parenting, work, and overscheduled lives.

So I've shared some of our e-mails, hoping that they will help you understand what the lives of military families can be like. (Of course, I know most military spouses out there are a lot more competent, organized, and on top of things than I've ever been.)

I hope I make you laugh some, and maybe cry a little, too. Because tears are necessary, but laughter gets us through it.

Thank you for reading this book. If it gives you insight into the lives of military families, please say thank you to one. We make these sacrifices out of love for our spouses, our country, and the American people.

> *Alesia Holliday, October 2002*
> *Seattle . . . for now.*

# Glossary of Military and Navy Jargon

**BOQ**—Bachelor Officers' Quarters

**CAC**—Combat Air Crew, a P-3's crew; works together throughout deployment.

**CO**—Commanding Officer, the head of a squadron

**CDR**—Commander, a naval rank (0-5)

**Deployment**—A period of time during which a squadron is sent away to serve in foreign lands or seas

**Detailer**—A person assigned to match job needs in the Navy with the people who fill them. (Detailers are the people who decide who gets stationed, or assigned, where and when.)

**DOD**—Department of Defense

**OSC**—Officers' Spouses' Club, a social organization for military spouses. There are also Enlisted Spouses' Clubs.

**Prowler**—A variant of the A-6 Intruder, an all-weather attack airplane of the 1960s and 1970s. The EA-6B operates from land or an aircraft carrier, is specifically designed for electronic attack, and is used to disrupt and disable enemy air defense. The normal crew consists of four members with various duties.

**P-3 Orion**—Land-based, turbo-prop aircraft originally designed for maritime patrol and antisubmarine warfare. Based on the commercial plane the Lockheed Electra, the P-3 entered Navy service in 1963. Production of the aircraft stopped in the late 1980s, and no replacement currently exists. The normal crew consists of eleven members with various duties. (Judd's plane.)

# Glossary of Military and Navy Jargon

**Ready, or The Ready**—Designates a crew and an aircraft to be on short notice standby to support a particular mission, usually Search and Rescue. The crew is often required to remain together and/or in their quarters for the duration of their Ready status.

**SNAFU**—Situation Normal, All Fouled Up

**Squadron**—A unit of organization in naval aviation. A Patrol Squadron consists of nine or ten aircraft and approximately four hundred personnel. The P-3 squadron is a subunit of a Patrol Wing, which consists of three Patrol Squadrons under the administrative command of a Navy Captain given the title Commodore.

**Squids**—A slang term for ship sailors or Navy personnel in general, usually used only by fellow squids

**Standing Duty**—Periodically an aircrew is required to perform the administrative functions for the Squadron. These usually consist of twenty-four-hour watches as Squadron Duty Officer (SDO) or Assistant SDO. The SDO is tasked with the day-to-day administrative functions and with ensuring that the CO is kept apprised of current aircraft and aircrew status.

**VADM**—Vice Admiral, a naval rank (0-9)

**VP-40**—Judd's squadron on Whidbey Island, Washington.

**XO**—Executive Officer, the second-in-command in a squadron

If you marry someone in the military, you have to be ready for anything. After four years, three states, and two children, I thought I was. Then came deployment.

# Chapter 1

## *It's Not Just a Marriage, It's an Adventure*

**To:** Judd
**From:** Alesia
**Subject:** You're gone even though you're still here.

I think I'm having some kind of weird culture shock. Oak Harbor is so very much a Navy town. The base is the center of everything, and there are Navy people everywhere. Driving through town today, I passed signs and banners saying good-bye to you—BE SAFE, VP-40 FIGHTING MARLINS—and hello to the returning squadron.

I am e-mailing you even though you haven't left yet, because I never see you when you're awake. This pre-deployment workup stuff is pretty intense. I'm not sure I would have moved here with you from Florida, if I'd known I'd never see you. I can't believe you had to work the day the movers brought our furniture and our household goods. You can imagine how much fun it was trying to keep Connor occupied, breast-feed Lauren under a blanket in the driveway, and direct the movers which room to put what box in, all at the same time.

This takes "multitasking" to a whole new level.

p.s. I saw a coyote. IN OUR YARD.

I truly believe that one of the detailers has a really sick sense of humor. This is the detailer who always gets Judd's name, of course.

For example, our first Navy move as a married couple was from Columbus, Ohio, to Pensacola, Florida, when I was seven months pregnant and about the same size as an average battleship. So we settled in to life in Pensacola, where all the Navy's flight training goes on.

I say "settled in" as a shorthand for: Judd performed bizarre rituals like sitting in a room and playing games while all the oxygen was sucked out of the room, and escaping from a helicopter into which he was strapped, blindfolded, *at the bottom of a pool, on purpose.* Meanwhile, I had the excitement of fire-breathing indigestion and my skeleton literally coming unglued that only the eight- and nine-months pregnant woman can really appreciate.

For the first time in my life, I had no job, no friends nearby, and I lived more than an easy day's drive from my family. I was miserable for a while. Then, as it generally does, life got better and Pensacola was a pretty wonderful few years.

Enter Evil Detailer again. "Hey, she's pregnant. We need to make them move, quick!"

Our second move, after some "split living"—Judd moved to Texas and then Jacksonville, Florida, for different schools and training, while I stayed in Pensacola with Connor, and we visited every weekend (except during the hurricanes)—was from Florida to Washington State. About as far across the country as you can get.

This time, we had a two-and-a-half-year-old who was only a few weeks out of diapers and a three-and-a-half-week-old infant. So, naturally, we decided to drive across the country.

With the children.

In two separate cars.

In hindsight, it wasn't our smartest idea. It took seven ten-hour days to make that trip, and it was the longest week of my life. Crossing Oklahoma took about three years. We had to stop at least seventy-nine times a day. We would just get started and Connor would say, "I have to go potty. *Now.*" You don't tell a two-year-old to hold it. So we would stop at a rest stop, take him potty, get snacks from the vending machine, and start off again.

Five miles later, the baby would wake up and howl to be breast-fed. Babies aren't really known for their patience, either. Especially not Lauren. She's a *feed me now* kind of girl. So we stopped again, nursed the baby (I nursed the baby, actually; Judd refused to help at all), made Connor go potty (just in case), and started up again.

Ten miles later, one of us would need to get gas.

Picture this continuing for 3,500 miles.

If I don't make it to Heaven when I die, I know I'll wake up back on that road trip. We tried everything. We tried to synchronize Connor's naptimes with the baby's. (Ha!) We tried coordinating gas fill-ups, but the cars used fuel at different rates just to spite us.

My sweet sister-in-law, Megan, had volunteered to help us drive. (She's single with no kids; poor thing didn't know any better.) Two years later, she still hasn't recovered.

While Megan drove my car, I tried to figure out how to breast-feed while I was still seatbelted and Lauren was in her car seat. Trust me, you'd need six-foot-long breasts and a time-out from the laws of physics for that one to work. So, we stopped.

And we stopped.

And we stopped.

Finally, we reached our new home on Whidbey Island. Sort of. We needed to find a house to rent, so we spent about six weeks in a tiny motel where the heat didn't work properly. We slept in the Sahara, but went to the bathroom in Siberia.

In my sleep-deprived haze, I kept muttering things like, "I didn't sign up for this. I never went to boot camp. I didn't sign on any dotted line. I didn't enlist. I never wanted to Be All That I Could Be. I don't Aim High."

Judd just smiled, waved our marriage license and the kids' birth certificates in front of my bloodshot eyes, and said quietly, "It's Not Just a Marriage, It's an Adventure."

I hate people who have to have the last word.

# Chapter 2

## *Departure: Only 183 Days to Go*

**To:** Judd
**From:** Alesia
**Subject:** Thank you for the flowers, you stinker!!

Some beautiful yellow roses were delivered to the house when I was outside painting this afternoon—you wouldn't know anything about that, would you? I love you, silly man.

Everybody keeps calling me to see if I'm OK. It's funny, but I'm just fine. I guess I'm so used to our commuter lifestyle that it doesn't feel out of the ordinary to have you gone for a couple of days. I figure at about three weeks it'll hit me hard, and I'll fall apart. We painted and played outside and read a zillion books. It was a pretty great day, other than the fact you weren't here to share it (which is big). Connor asked me at bedtime where you were; he wanted you to read him some books. I explained again, and we watched the video of you reading a story. He seemed OK with it.

**To:** Alesia
**From:** Judd
**Subject:** re: Thank you

Hi, sweetie. I've had a lot of difficulties finding a phone to call you on in Atsugi. I didn't get a chance to go into Tokyo. My buddy Andy Perez didn't get his bags back from the plane until late, so we just sat in the BOQ and watched rugby. I'm glad you got and enjoyed the flowers! I love you very much! We will be leaving here in a few hours and going to Kadena, Japan, which is on the island of Okinawa. From there, we go to Utapao, Thailand. Not too much jet lag. Please hug and kiss the kids for me. I suppose you can pet the dog, too. I love you!!

**To:** Judd
**From:** Alesia
**Subject:** Still OK, stop worrying!

I got your phone message. Stop worrying! So I'm alone with a baby and a two-year-old. I'm a tough trial lawyer, how hard can staying at home with two kids be? [NOTE TO SELF: The stupidest thing I've ever said in my entire life.] I don't even have to wear pantyhose!!

I had the going-away party for the OSC here at the house today. It was great to meet everyone. I don't remember many names, of course, but everyone was so friendly. Your CO's wife, Carrie, and the

XO's wife, Robin, were the last ones to leave, so I got a chance to talk with them a little. They're terrific! Connor had so much fun with all the kids. He ran up and down our hill so much today that, when he tried to stand up after dinner, he fell back down, looked at me with a comical expression of surprise, and said, "Mommy, my legs are broked!"

We miss you a lot and, I have to admit, after the conversations I took part in and overheard today, I'm a little worried. The spouses who have been through many deployments were pretty grim. Many of them were already in tears (especially the ones whose husbands just left in the airlift today). Maybe this is going to be worse than I thought.

But I know we'll be fine. So take care of yourself and write me lots of e-mails and tell me all about the heat and the people and the wonderful sights you're seeing!! You know I wish I could be going along for the adventure. (I know; I'll go there and YOU study for the Washington bar exam.)

p.s. Try not to get emotionally attached to any camels.

No matter how courageous, strong, and self-sufficient you are—and military spouses are among the bravest people I have ever known—weeks or months of being a single parent, while envisioning your spouse acting as a human missile target, is a pretty tough job. I, known more for self-confidence than intelligence, was sure I'd be just fine.

Boy, did I have a lot to learn.

When we moved to Whidbey Island, I learned one of the scariest words in the English language: *deployment.*

Just whisper the word in any gathering of military spouses, and a shudder of horror will race through the room. Storm clouds will gather on foreheads. People will tell horror stories in hushed voices: "Then Hurricane Andrew hit, and we had to evacuate. I was in the hospital having my appendix out, and had to drag the baby, the boys, and the dog up to Georgia with the IV pole still strapped to my arm and the doctor tied down to the luggage rack. *By myself.*"

"He was due back on October 6, which would have been six months on the dot, but the planes broke down in the squadron replacing him, so he was stuck in Turkey for another *nineteen days.*"

"I once went twenty-five days, seven hours, and thirty-three minutes without hearing *one word.*"

Trust me, none of this is exaggeration. (OK, maybe the appendix thing. Sort of.)

Enduring freedom and enduring love. The Navy ship sails over the horizon, or the Air Force plane flies off into the sunset. CNN broadcasts these patriotic images into homes across America, showing the spouses of servicemen and women waving flags and smiling bravely, as their loved ones leave for up to half a year of separation. Such courage, such fortitude, such calm and stoic acceptance of the sacrifices they must endure. Then the cameras stop rolling.

The real story is more like this: Four hours of waiting in the hangar or on the dock has pushed you three hours past the two-year-old's naptime. The cookies and punch that someone with no kids so thoughtfully provided has the five-year-old hopped-up on a sugar high that will last until a week from Tuesday. The baby has a look on her face that says the jet that just took off with Daddy inside wasn't the only thing on the runway filled with gas. The cell phone shows you missed three calls—two from your secretary and one from your boss. You finally get everyone strapped in the various car seats, but realize the car is out of gas. You pass a McDonald's on the way to the gas station, and everyone in the car sets up a simultaneous howling. You feel like joining them and think: "Only 183 days to go," as you start laughing like a crazy person.

Welcome to the world of the military spouse.

# Chapter 3

## The Stay-at-Home Military Spouse

**To:** Judd
**From:** Alesia
**Subject:** I found out how hard it can be.

I can't believe I ever thought being a stay-at-home Mom was easy. My worst day in the middle of trial prep was easier than this! I never even get a coffee break. No leisurely lunches with friends. I don't even get to go to the bathroom by myself!

My day today basically sucked. I had to rush around getting the kids ready, so we could get Connor to preschool on time. This was picture day, so the teacher wanted all the parents to come in. That took an hour, and the place was a zoo with all the parents, so by then Lauren was very tired and whiny. Connor said he wanted to leave, but they had some program he was rehearsing for, so he decided to stay at school while we ran to the grocery. Of course, Lauren fell asleep in the car and woke up when we got to the store, so instead of her usual hour and a half nap, she had twenty minutes in the car. You can imagine how cheerful she was in the grocery store. Sigh.

Then it was already time to pick Connor up. When I walked in, the teacher said, "Didn't you get our message? Connor vomited all over the place five minutes after you left." They thought he just ate his snack too fast and choked a little, because he was fine five minutes later. We took our bag of vomit clothes and got back in the car.

In a stroke of brilliant planning and foresight, I had previously scheduled a portrait session at Sears for this very afternoon! So I had to drive clear over to Burlington and try to get two tired, cranky children to smile. Connor wouldn't do it. He is very clingy these days and keeps saying "I miss my Daddy." I don't know what to tell him. I miss you, too.

I think I might be losing my mind.

In more news of my "how hard can it be" day, I finally got the kids home, fed, and to bed. Then I had to clean up the dinner dishes, figure out whether or not I had missed my amoxycillin dose (I took it again, what the heck), start the dishwasher, clean up the mud Connor tracked in, clean up the bathroom from bath time, take out the garbage and decide what to do since we're out of trash bags, take the dog out on the leash because he keeps trying to run away (so fun, when it's 40 degrees outside), change the sheets on my bed from where Lauren peed through her diaper, start a load of laundry, and make a list of things to do tomorrow.

In my spare time.

I got your e-mail. If you ask me whether I got the lawn mower attachments one more time, I swear I will throw the thing off Deception Pass Bridge and buy a goat. I promise I will get to the lawn mower store when I get a minute!!

OK, it's only midnight. I think I'll finally go take my morning shower.

**To:** Alesia
**From:** Judd
**Subject:** I will never say LAWN MOWER again.

I'm sorry you are having a tough time. I hope you are feeling better. We have been flying every day, all day long, so I haven't had a chance to check e-mail. I hope Connor is just going through a phase, and isn't too stressed out from my leaving. I have been sending sleepy vibes to Lauren to make her sleep through at least part of the night for you.

I am very proud of you for organizing and hosting the OSC's squadron going-away party. I know you feel like you're in the Twilight Zone sometimes, but you're doing great! It is still pretty hot here (big surprise!), especially after having to wait out in the sun for the bus. It has gotten windy, so you collect dust and grit on your clothes and in your eyes and mouth. We flew around the Arabian Gulf all night looking at stuff. It was pretty calm and boring, which is a good thing. I'm going to get some sleep before we fly again tonight. Judd-the-Dusty

**To:** Judd
**From:** Alesia
**Subject:** I've lost my identity.

It's the weirdest sensation, but I feel like my identity has disappeared. I have become The Invisible Woman.

To shop at the commissary, I have to show my "dependent" ID card. (I haven't been "dependent" on anyone since I was a child.) To take the kids to the doctor, I have to give *your* name and *your* Social Security number. Even the veterinarian's receptionist I called today for P.J.'s shots asked—and keep in mind that this was the office of a *woman* vet—"What is your husband's name?"

I said, "What?"

"We set up all the files under the husband's name."

You can imagine how well I took that. I said, "What if I don't *have* a husband? Do I have to go somewhere ELSE for my dog's care??"

I used a different vet.

But, it's insidious. At social gatherings, the first thing you usually do when you meet someone new is ask "What do you do?" Not anymore. Now the first thing anybody asks me is, "What does your *husband* do?" Or, what squadron are *you* in?

To understand how odd this feels to me, switch it around. Imagine if the first things anybody asked *you* were, "What does your wife do? What law firm are *you* in?"

Today, at the mall, I thought I had a reprieve from all this anonymity. Connor started chatting with a guy when we were in line for ice cream, and the guy asked him, "What does your Mommy do?"

Finally! Someone cares what I do! OK, it was a total stranger trying to be nice to a talkative kid, but I'll take what I can get. I waited breathlessly for Connor to say: "This is my Mommy, she takes care of me and baby sister." Or: "Mommy's a lawyer, she helps people." Two pretty important jobs, right?

Connor took a deep breath, looked at me, then up at the man, and said proudly: "Mommy breaks things and Daddy fixes them."

# Chapter 4

## *It's Tuesday, What Time Is It in Bahrain?*

**June 2000**

**To:** Alesia
**From:** Judd
**Subject:** Still hot here

We flew all last night, training another crew. We got to see both a sunset and a sunrise. Breakfast is pretty interesting here; raw eggs, dates, and olives. It takes a little getting used to. Thanks again for the Father's Day package and pictures. I was the envy of everyone, since mine actually came on time! I can't believe how big Lauren is getting!

I am absolutely on the best crew I could have gotten. Everyone works great together and enjoys hanging out when we aren't flying, too.

The computer keeps kicking me offline, so I will go stand in line to try to call you in a little bit. I think it's around bedtime for you, so I hope you're still up.

**To:** Judd
**From:** Alesia
**Subject:** It's OK that you called and woke me up.

I can't get the time difference straight, either. Just when I get it figured out, we hit daylight savings time, or you move to a different country. (That sounds weird—It's Wednesday, what country is Judd in?) Connor can find Madagascar and Bahrain on a map now, but has no idea where Ohio is.

**To:** Alesia
**From:** Judd
**Subject:** Leaving again

The flight went very well and the Admiral seemed happy with us (a happy Admiral is always a good thing). Unfortunately, as soon as we stepped off the aircraft, we were told that we had to pack up and go to "a different country," as you put it, tomorrow morning. Nobody is all that thrilled, but we go where they need us. I hear there's not much e-mail or phone access there, so I'll be in touch when I can. I'll try to call you tomorrow morning (tonight for you, I think). I have to go pack and find something to eat. Talk to you soon!

**To:** Judd
**From:** Alesia
**Subject:** Sorry I missed your call.

I guess I'll hear from you when I hear from you. It's so upsetting when I miss your call one of the few times you get to a phone, but I've found myself hibernating in the house hoping the phone will ring (which is *not* a good thing, unlike a happy Admiral), and cabin fever is driving us all nuts. So I'll just e-mail and pretend you're going to read it sometime soon. We miss you so much, and I can't believe we won't see you until almost Christmas. It occurred to me today that six months is actually HALF A YEAR. Somehow, that sounds much worse.

**To:** Alesia
**From:** Judd
**Subject:** We're back!

And I can finally get your e-mails. Don't think of it as half a year; that sounds like forever. Just think of it as only about 22 more weeks. I'm going to get a phone card and call as soon as I figure out what time it is in Seattle. No more waking you up in the middle of the night!

E-mail to the Front

**To:** Judd
**From:** Alesia
**Subject:** You have to admit, it IS pretty funny!

The first nap I've taken with the kids in three weeks . . . RING!!!! It's like washing my car to make it rain. Whenever I want you to call, I'm going to fall asleep! We miss you, too, and the kids are looking forward to the stuffed camels.

# Chapter 5

## *The Dreaded Paper Chain*

**June 2000**

**To:** Judd
**From:** Alesia
**Subject:** I have construction paper taped to my butt.

I had a bright idea to make a paper chain with one link representing every day you were gone. That way, Connor could tear off a link every day, and it would be a tangible symbol for him of the fact you are coming back.

Let me point out that a just-turned three-year-old has the attention span of a gnat. He lasted all of 17 links and was done. Mommy got to stay up till midnight, cutting and gluing paper links together. Of course, I put in about 20 extra, since we don't know the exact date you'll be back, and I don't want to run out. Do you know what half a year looks like in paper-chain land???? I have the darn thing strung up all around the room, like some kind of giant purple and green fungus. At about 100 links or so, I gave up on beauty and got out the stapler. Things moved along a little quicker then!

**To:** Alesia
**From:** Judd
**Subject:** Paper chains & other stuff

The paper chain sounds like a great idea! Take a picture so I can see it. (Responding to 5 e-mails here; been flying all the time.) Yes, you can plug the piano into the wall with the adapter. You need to check the oil in the mower *every time* you use it. There are lines on the dipstick to tell you how much is left. If you need to add oil, use 5W-30 motor oil, or get lawn mower oil at the hardware store. Don't add the whole thing, just add enough to bring it up to the proper level.

I'm sorry Connor is so sad. I miss him too. I sent a postcard just for him and hope it arrives soon. I miss you all VERY VERY much, and it makes me grumpy to be away.

The weather here is getting hotter! The air-conditioning shuts off around 2 a.m., so I wake up by 2:30 when the room temperature reaches 97 degrees. The cabdriver said, "You think it's hot now, wait till August. You'll wish you were dead."

It wasn't really encouraging.

I hope you are all getting some rest today. I can't wait to hear Lauren practicing her new laugh!

**To:** Judd
**From:** Alesia
**Subject:** What is it with your kids and artificial nipples?

Lauren is just like Connor. I can't get her to take a bottle for anything. I went to the store and bought one of every kind of different bottle and nipple they had, thinking maybe she would have some sort of preference (the bottle manufacturers are all trying to replicate Mommy now, very forward-thinking, but your daughter is Not Fooled).

If I could get her to take a bottle, I could have a baby-sitter for a few hours once in a while and take a Mommy Mental Health break and see a movie or just sit in the park and read a book. Everyone needs at least an hour or two a week to herself.

Even Mommies.

Hugs, Alesia the human milk truck

**To:** Alesia
**From:** Judd
**Subject:** Please don't send me e-mail with the word nipple in the subject line.

Remember, I usually have to use a computer in a room filled with lots of guys. I may never live this down.

When I get home, you can take days and days of mental health breaks and see all the movies and read all the books you want. I promise.

Kids who don't yet understand the difference between "yesterday" and "last Thursday" are not going to comprehend what six months means. The first deployment lasted more than half of Lauren's life, and almost a quarter of Connor's, to put it in perspective. We tried to do things that made the time manageable, like the paper chain. We also crossed days off on the calendar, and sent Daddy a box of presents every week. But, in a long deployment, these tactics can almost be counterproductive. The sheer size of the paper chain overwhelmed and depressed us. It wasn't until we made it through fifty or sixty links that we felt as if we might actually see Judd again some day.

Young children don't understand at all. They just know they miss Daddy and they want him to come home and wrestle, read books, and go to the park. As hard as I tried, I could never get the "voices" right when I read the bedtime books (Daddy does all the characters). I didn't know what the "broccoli song" was. We tried to explain in the days leading up to deployment, and over and over again while Judd was gone, but they were just too young. All Connor and, later, Lauren knew was that they were hurting and angry and sad. When I had to face the fact that I couldn't fix it—I couldn't make them *not* miss Daddy—it was the hardest lesson I've ever had to learn as a parent.

My friends with older children say the reactions are different, but the emotions are the same. The kids understand intellectually that Mommy or Daddy has to be gone, and why, and for how long. But none of that understanding makes up for the missed championship soccer game or piano recital. Or even for ordinary family dinners and homework.

So military families try to love their kids a little more. And cherish them a bit more. And spend more time together, when we're not on different hemispheres. We try to explain and console, fix the boo-boos, and cuddle the sadness away.

Just like every other parent does, I guess. We're not that different, after all.

# Chapter 6

## *The Lawn Mower SNAFU*

**June 2000**

**To:** Judd
**From:** Alesia
**Subject:** The lawn mower is not working.

06/02: We just bought this thing before you left and there is no reason why it shouldn't work. Maybe I need to change the oil?

------------------------------------------

06/03: I got your e-mail about the little rubber button on the rear of the engine and pumping it. What does "prime the fuel in the mower" mean? Also, is there a correct number of times to pump the button? I pumped it at least 35 times, but it didn't seem to help.

------------------------------------------

06/04: It's not really fair to expect me to know about flooding the engine, if you don't tell me. I'll go try again.

------------------------------------------

06/05: It still doesn't work. I really think I need to change the oil.

------------------------------------------

06/06: How would I know if the spark-plug wire is loose from the top of the spark plug???? I didn't even know that lawn mowers HAD spark plugs.

---
06/07: What's a spark plug?

---
06/08: I changed the oil. I even turned the mower upside down to make sure all the oil drained out. Then I put fresh, new oil in it. I asked the guy at the shop, so I know I got the right kind. I filled it to the top.

---
06/09: Evidently I wasn't supposed to put so much oil in the mower. The smoke went away fairly quickly, though. Connor even got to go for a ride in the fire truck.

---
06/10: This is ridiculous! We paid good money for this mower and nothing works. Our grass is so long, I think I saw leopards and orangutans wandering around. I am taking it back to the shop. If they think they can sell me a defective mower, they are seriously mistaken. I am not some meek person who will put up with this. I will sue them for fraud. I am taking it back first thing tomorrow morning.

---
06/11: Apparently lawn mowers need gasoline.

Most married people develop a comfortable system of who does what. It's a big part of the reason for getting married in the first place. We all have different strengths and preferences.

He's a gourmet cook; she thinks microwave mac and cheese was a great invention. She does the gardening; he cleans the garage. After a few years of marriage, it becomes a seamless process.

Unless you're a military spouse.

Once deployment starts, the whole system ends up in the garbage. Which *you* now have to take out, by the way.

In our marriage, the lawn is firmly on Judd's side of the balance sheet. I'm allergic to everything green and growing; he worked in a nursery (the plant kind, not the baby kind) to help pay for college. So it just makes sense that I never had to do anything in the way of yard work.

Then came deployment.

We had a nice, sensible apartment in Florida. A lawn service came once a week, at about 5 A.M., and woke us up by firing up weed whackers underneath our bedroom window. Normal city life, in other words.

Then we moved to Washington (state of, not DC) and into a house with a lawn the approximate size of Yosemite national forest. We actually had deer wandering around our backyard eating berries off the bushes. Most people would think, "How lovely. Whidbey Island is so beautiful and unspoiled, we have deer roaming from the forest into our yard."

I thought, "How wonderful. Deer poop."

*Note:* It is a basic law of physics that one six-inch pile of steaming deer poop located anywhere in a five-acre yard will be found and stepped in by any child worth her $79 Nikes.

So, faced with the deer-infested yard, and being unemployed and frugal, I decided to mow the lawn myself. Planning the logistics of Mowing Day was something like Patton planning the invasion of Sicily. Only *he* had help.

First, I had to find something to occupy Connor, so he didn't get anywhere near the lawn mower. It's important to know that tiny boys are irresistibly attracted to anything with a dangerous engine that might potentially chop an arm or leg off. Also, Child Protective Services frowns on tying children to the porch railing.

Or so I've heard.

Then, I had to determine the range of the nursery monitor and map the areas where trees, hills, or the neighbor's karaoke machine would knock out the transmission.

Finally, Lauren had to take a nap. During the daylight. When it wasn't raining. This is easier said than done in Washington.

After accomplishing all pre-mission tasks, I began the actual mowing.

I am very proud to report that three days, two boxes of allergy medication, seven broken fingernails, and three temper tantrums later (only one of which was mine), I paid a neighbor kid $50 to mow the other two-thirds of the lawn.

The deer poop still hasn't come out of my shoes.

# Chapter 7

## *You're Off Saving the World, and I'm Home Cleaning Up Dog Vomit*

**To:** Alesia
**From:** Judd
**Subject:** The Bahrain Hard Rock Café

We were flying again last night and worked with a British Royal Navy ship. One of the people talking to me on the radio was obviously from Scotland and had a very heavy accent. I'm sure he was saying the same thing about me!

We went to the Hard Rock Café in Bahrain for dinner (absolutely not like any Hard Rock we've ever seen, picture a bunch of people in turbans eating burgers). I had a BBQ Lamb sandwich (their "most popular sandwich") and, as you might expect, I have an upset stomach. I think I just need to get used to stuff and am going to try some new foods the next time we go out. In the meantime, you might want to mail me some Pepto-Bismol.

Priority mail.

**To:** Judd
**From:** Alesia
**Subject:** It's been one of those days.

When you wake up and step in dog yark the moment you get out of bed, and that was the high point of your day, you're in big trouble.

I read your e-mail about flying with the British Navy and talking to some Scottish guy over the radio. I wonder if his wife wants to escape and move to Mexico, too? We could be beach buddies . . .

And the Bahrain Hard Rock Café sounds fun, too. Probably not a lot of women in Harley tank tops? We had lunch at the exotic Whidbey Island McDonald's. Gourmet chicken McSomethings.

P.J. keeps trying to make a break for the hills every time we go out, even with me standing right there. He's a city boy, and all this wilderness is messing with his tiny doggy mind. He sort of sidles off, glancing at me out of the corner of his eye, like I won't notice. Much to his dismay, I send his butt back to the house. One taste of freedom, and suddenly he's Jack Kerouac. Next he'll be wearing a little leather jacket and singing biker-dog songs.

The neighbor said we have CANNIBALISTIC COYOTES around here who have actually EATEN some neighborhood dogs. Are you getting this?? You moved me to the wilderness. *Me*, the woman who considers "roughing it" to be a hotel without room service,

in a place with deer poop all over the place and
pet-eating coyotes.

I have decided that I'm not what you would call
a domestic goddess. The house looks like very
messy burglars ransacked the place. I am pretty
much too tired to care—Lauren had me up four times
during the night. Another growth spurt, they tell
me. She is going to weigh 600 pounds and be 12
feet tall, at this rate. When we finally got to
sleep at 5 a.m., Connor decided it was time to get
up for the day.

I am shipping you the children—watch for a box
with airholes in it.

**To:** Alesia
**From:** Judd
**Subject:** Still sick

We are back in Bahrain and just finished moving
into the barracks this morning. I'm feeling pretty
miserable, since I have a cold now. Sneezing,
coughing, and stuffed-up head. If it gets worse,
they'll down me from flying. Things are pretty
busy here. We had another flight last night. When
we get back, we usually have another two- to
three-hour debrief. Along with the three- to four-
hour preflight, it is usually about a 15-hour day
or more. I miss you so much and am sorry you're
so tired. Give Connor and Lauren lots of hugs and
kisses from me!

**To:** Judd
**From:** Alesia
**Subject:** Guilt trips and other journeys

I am scum. I'm complaining about stepping in dog vomit, when you're off saving the world. I'm sorry. I just get so wrapped up in exhaustion some days. I hope your cold is better and you get some rest.

Please know I am so proud of you for what you're doing. We talk about Daddy every day and blow kisses to your picture every night. The kids love and miss you. Talk to you soon.

# Chapter 8

## *I Don't Churn My Own Butter, Either*

**July 2000**

**To:** Judd
**From:** Alesia
**Subject:** Learning to be on our own

We are getting into a routine and figuring out life without Daddy. It is pretty sad around here in the evenings and on Sunday, though. Sundays are always the worst, for some reason. The lack of routine, I guess, plus Sunday was always our laze around with the whole family day.

We went to church today, and I was brave enough to leave Lauren in the nursery for almost 14 whole minutes. It's the longest I've ever been away from her. NOTE TO SELF: I really need to get a life.

After church, I decided to let Connor "swim." It's a beautiful, sunny day here. So I inflated his little pool, put on his sunscreen, filled the pool with warm water on the patio, and made a "tent" between two chairs with a sheet for the tent and a beach towel for him to sit on. He was so happy!

I went inside for 30 seconds to get Popsicles, keeping an eye on him through the screen door and window. When I came back outside, an amazing sight greeted me: a naked boy mooning me from inside the tent, as he arranged his towel just so. I asked, "Connor, why did you take your swimsuit off?"

He looked at me like I was a complete idiot: "Mommy, I didn't want to get my towel wet."

In other exciting news bulletins, Lauren had her first green beans today and, right on schedule, had her first green beans poop shortly thereafter. It was truly nasty, yet even *I* can't believe my life is reduced to e-mailing you halfway around the world about green baby poop. This must violate some kind of international treaty.

I went to a spouses' meeting, and every single person in that room is coping with all of this much better than I am. I felt like a total loser. One woman brought homemade chocolate fudge that she was up till 3 a.m. making. She said she threw out the first two batches, because the sweetness-to-chocolate ratio wasn't just right. I'm not kidding.

I brought a tray of cookies I picked up at Albertson's on the way. The sweetness-to-cellophane ratio seemed fine to me.

The hostess's house was perfect, too. It looked like something out of *Home and Gardens,* while ours looks like the "before" picture in an ad for house-cleaning services. It was very depressing. (I did console myself with three pieces of homemade fudge, though.) The whole experience made me want to learn to cook, or bake, or at least churn my own butter.

In my continuing slide into life as a bad sitcom, I went out for some "retail therapy" afterward. I had a makeover and spent more on makeup than I did on my first car.

p.s. When does that combat pay thing kick in?

**To:** Alesia
**From:** Judd
**Subject:** Green bean poop

You have no idea how reading an e-mail about green poop braces a man to go off to battle.

p.s. By the way, just how much did your first car cost?

One of my big problems on the first deployment was that I was secretly convinced that everyone else was managing better than I was. It was so reassuring to talk to other people like me who loved their kids more than life itself, yet also wanted to change their names from Mommy to something else. Fred, for example. Of course, when I tried this on Connor, he never missed a beat. "Freeeeeeeed, can I have a juice pop now?"

You learn to cherish the little accomplishments. At the park one day, one of Connor's friends said to me, while we all sat around and played in the sand, "You're the only Mommy who gets dirty!" I considered this to be high praise. I want my kids to remember me as a fun Mom who played with them, not as the woman whose house was always spotless. Especially when we were all coping with missing Daddy so much.

So, no, I didn't churn my own butter. My house usually had toys, books, and games strewn all over. But, you know what? It's OK. I'd write more, but I have to go build a tent.

# Chapter 9

## *My Nomination for Mother of the Year Got Lost*

**To:** Judd
**From:** Alesia
**Subject:** I am a terrible mother.

Connor was cranky all morning and afternoon, and he wouldn't nap. I actually gave him his first spanking. He was being a total monster, and when I tried to put him in the Time Out chair for a little break, he hit, pinched, and bit me. So I swatted his little behind once.

Then I burst into tears.

He's acting out so badly, and I don't know what to do. At least four times a day he says, "Mommy, don't ever leave me," or "Don't leave me like Daddy did." It's awful.

So, now I am officially a child beater and should surrender my right to be a parent and give myself up to the proper authorities. I don't think I've ever disliked myself so much.

We had a talk then and much cuddling and hugging. I think seeing me cry upset him much more than the smack (which he didn't actually seem to feel), and so we cried together a bit. I told him that I miss Daddy, too, but we need to be nice to each other.

**To:** Alesia
**From:** Judd
**Subject:** You are a wonderful mother.

I'm sorry that Connor is taking this so hard. I will try and call you soon, so at least I can talk to him on the phone. I know it's so tough for him to understand why Daddy's gone. I'm using the camera you sent to have everybody take pictures of me doing the things I do in a day, so Connor can have a scrapbook of Daddy. It's a great idea and maybe it will help. Talk to you soon.

**To:** Judd
**From:** Alesia
**Subject:** Separation anxiety

The separation anxiety around here is amazing. Connor cries when I take him to preschool, but when we talked about quitting preschool and staying home with Mommy on those three mornings a week, he cried and said he wanted to go to school. I am pretty much at my wits' end.

He has learned new expressions at school, too. This week he learned the word GROSS. Everything is gross. He yelled in from the living room the other night: Chicken is GROSS. I started laughing so hard; it was just so funny and unexpected. Now, of course, it's every other word. I wonder what other exciting words he'll bring home?

## E-mail to the Front

Lauren had a busy and productive day rolling from her back to her tummy. She really hates being on her stomach, so it's pretty amusing. She manages to roll on her tummy, looks all around, and gets really ticked off. Then she either starts howling, so I flip her on to her back (at which point it starts all over) or she figures out, "Hey, I know how to roll back over again!" and does that.

There's a grim determination to it all, like she's got a job to do. She's going to roll on her tummy 50 times a day or else. Baby punching the development time clock. It's fascinating to watch. She is so beautiful she takes my breath away.

I made cookies to take over to P.J.'s home-away-from-home to thank the woman for rescuing him TWICE after he ran off. Did I tell you that there are roving packs of coyotes around here that have been known to attack neighborhood pets? Also, raccoons with no fear who actually came through the doggie door into the neighbor's garage and raided the dog food. Great. Just call me Grizzly Alesia. Maybe I can start trapping whales and harpooning beavers for a hobby.

I'll send you new pictures of the kids, as soon as you send me directions on how to get this digital camera to work. I really bring the phrase "mechanically challenged" to a whole new level, don't I?

We are trying a new routine of having special Connor-and-Mommy time now. Every time Lauren goes for a nap, we get out the "special" bag of toys and games. Connor gets to choose one, and we just play together for 20-30 minutes. I'm not getting a thing done around the house, but it is helping him a lot.

Doing laundry is so overrated, anyway.

# Chapter 10

## *Lattes and Diet Coke Transfusions*

**July 2000**

**To:** Judd
**From:** Alesia
**Subject:** This is how cults brainwash people.

They make them stay awake for days and days at a time, and then make them shave their heads, eat tofu cupcakes, and ask total strangers for money.

Sign me up. They've got to get more sleep than I do. I could look good bald . . .

You're flying your check flight today, if I have the time change thing right and one of the ancient planes didn't die on you. I'm sending you good navigator vibes (sun rises in east and sets in west, remember—or is it different there? And remember, when in doubt, EJECT. 10-4, Roger, and all that stuff.)

I told Connor he had to help make my birthday cake this year, since you would be gone. He and I counted to my age together. He looked at me solemnly and said, "That's a lot of numbers, Mommy." <sigh> Don't I know it. He did tell me I'm his most beautiful girl, though. I love that kid.

We went to the art festival today. Then we were inspired, so we came home and painted a T-shirt for you. I'll ship it off to you tomorrow.

Connor's handprints came out great. In case you want to know what the green splotch is, Lauren wouldn't spread her fingers out, but got a death grip on the fabric instead. The so-called washable paint really isn't, so now they're both napping with green fingers. Not one of my better ideas, maybe, but it was fun!

**To:** Alesia
**From:** Judd
**Subject:** Good nav vibes

The check ride went very well. The good nav vibes you sent helped me immensely! I tried to call you but a ship pulled in to port and it is squid central here, so the lines for the phones are very long. We're going to go to the lovely grease pit called the "Dome" and eat some French Toast. We have the Ready tomorrow, so I will e-mail you more then.

I know how tired you must be. At least *we* have to have a required number of hours of sleep for flying. Too bad there's not a rule like that for Mommies!

p.s. Thanks for the cookies! I got TWO boxes from you the other day. Never seen so many jealous looks! I did share some, but ate all the chocolate-chip walnut ones myself.

**To:** Judd
**From:** Alesia
**Subject:** Life is good again—I have discovered Starbucks!

Coffee and caramel lattes. Life is worth living again. Also, on the way to Connor's gymnastics class, there's a drive-through espresso place that gives me a candy-covered coffee bean with my latte. If you look really pathetic and ask for extras, they give you a little baggie full of five or six candy-covered beans.

I drove through three times today.

So, when we got home, I vacuumed the house, dusted the furniture, bathed the kids, put them to sleep, washed the dishes, did a week's worth of laundry, sorted through ten years of accumulated photos and put them in albums, cleaned the oven, polished the hardwood floors, cleaned the bathrooms, and am now bouncing off the ceiling. Somehow—you guessed it—it's 3 a.m. again.

Maybe I'll cut down on the coffee beans.

# Chapter 11

## *Your Son Discovered His Penis This Week*

**To:** Judd
**From:** Alesia
**Subject:** YOU need to explain why girls don't have testicles.

Your son scared me to death today. He yelled for me at the top of his lungs from the bathroom, "Mommy, come quick, I have little balls in my peeper!" Of course, the first thing I thought, knowing Connor, is that he had somehow jammed the marbles from the Hungry Hippo game inside of his penis.

I made it to the bathroom in two seconds flat.

Connor was standing in front of the toilet, pants down around his ankles, looking extremely concerned. He was rolling his testicles around and looking at them. He turned enormous eyes to me:

"There's balls under here, Mommy."

"Those are your testicles, Connor, every boy has them." (Picture me holding in a laugh so huge my head starts turning purple.)

"Does Daddy have them?"

"Yes, Daddy has them. Daddy's are bigger." (I'm warning you, don't even go there.)

"Does P.J. have them?"

"Yes." (No way I'm getting into the concept of dog-neutering right now.)

"Do you have them?"

"No, I'm a girl, only boys have them."

"Does Baby Lauren have them?"

"No."

"Grandma?"

"No."

"When you grow up to be a Daddy, Mommy, will YOU have tecksickles?"

"No, I will never be a Daddy. I'm a girl."

"OK."

So, thus began genitalia appreciation week. It felt like the Discovery Channel around our house, except there were no water buffaloes mating.

"Mommy, why don't you have a penis?"

Well, Freud would say . . . No. Keep it simple.

"Only boys have penises."

"What do girls have?"

"Girls have vaginas."

"So, no penis AND no tecksickles, huh?" (Always a problem climbing the corporate ladder, too. Who knew it started at age two?)

"Right."

This became much more fun when Grandma was around, because I don't think my mother has ever said the word penis in her life. On one of our daily expeditions to Wal-Mart—really, the social hub of the island—Connor ambushed her.

Picture the tranquil setting of the Wal-Mart bathroom, and your son speaking to Grandma (who's in the next stall) in his usual soft, gentle voice that could out-decibel the average foghorn:

"Grandma, do you have a VAGINA?" (Sound of much laughter from other people in the bathroom and choking noises as Grandma swallowed her tongue.)

I stepped in to help, naturally.

"Yes, Connor, Grandma is a girl."

"Does she pee standing up?"

"No, she's a girl, she has to sit down."

"Because she has a VAGINA?"

"Yes, Connor." (Wishing the toilet would just open up and flush us through the floor.)

The bathroom is suddenly full of people. Wal-Mart is announcing a Roll-Back Pricing Special on potty humor in the women's bathroom.

"Grandma, when you grow up and you're a boy, you can pee standing up like me." (I just gave up completely at that point.)

"Connor, Daddy will tell you all about it on the phone tonight."

**To:** Alesia
**From:** Judd
**Subject:** I'm sorry you're mad at me.

I'm sorry I didn't want to discuss my son's testicles on the phone in the Ready Room, sur-rounded by 50 guys. Yes, I'm a wimp. I would have been tortured for months. It's just not happening.

**To:** Judd
**From:** Alesia
**Subject:** Peeing standing up is not as easy as you might think.

O.K., the problem is that the parent with the same equipment needs to be around for the whole demonstration process. I tried "aim at the floating Cheerios." He seems to be getting it.

**To:** Alesia
**From:** Judd
**Subject:** The Cheerios were a great idea.

I think some of the guys around here could use a few, especially after one too many beers. But that's another story . . .

# Chapter 12

## *Rebellion of the Appliances*

**July 2000**

**To:** Judd
**From:** Alesia
**Subject:** It's like a Stephen King novel around here.

The ongoing defection of the loyalty of the machines in this household continues. Yesterday, I was all set to mow, and the mower would not start. I may have told you this already. I'd just filled it with gas, anyway, and checked the oil (it has a cute little dipstick!) and everything looked fine. Grr.

I don't mean to be paranoid, but I swear they all knew the moment your plane lifted off the runway. The first sign was when the check engine light came on in the truck, *as I was driving it home from taking you to the hangar.* Don't tell *me* machines can't think.

So, I did the responsible, mature thing. I drove it for four more weeks, hoping the light would go off. (It didn't.) Anyway, we are lucky to have advanced computer diagnostics technology at the car dealers these days. It only cost us $300 for them to hook the truck up to a very smart computer, so the computer could tell the mechanic to tell us that the problem was the check engine light.

The light itself.

A $2.00 lightbulb.

The $300 was nonrefundable, of course. I swear I heard a sinister BWA HA HA HA emanating from the diagnostics machine as I drove off, but maybe the mechanic just got a bad burrito for lunch.

When I got home and tried to e-mail you, I turned on my computer to get one of my all-time favorite computer messages: "Fatal application error in sector #$%@^123 blah blah blah." I have no idea what that means, of course, but it can't be good, with the word FATAL in it. I called the computer company help desk and talked to the 12-year-old kid who runs the service department. He said I could mail it in to their priority service department in Bangladesh, but I'd be better off buying a new one. After all, we bought it seven months ago. It's practically a stone tablet and chisel. (Am using the laptop now.)

Mom was here for her visit by then, luckily, so she made us a nice roast beef dinner and said she would clean up the kitchen, so I could relax. She is the only human being on the planet who likes to wash dishes by hand, as she has told me 328 times. (I have a deep-seated character flaw because I use a dishwasher. This leads to me experiencing serious remorse for being a great disappointment as a daughter for almost two whole seconds before I load the dishwasher.) At least she stopped sniffing our refrigerator every time she comes to visit. And what normal person would WANT to eat off the kitchen floor????

Anyway, dinner wasn't all that relaxing, ulti-
mately, because Mom put the leftover roast down
the drain and turned on the garbage disposal.

Our garbage disposal has had several weeks to
become used to my cooking. In other words, almost
nothing goes down it but leftover macaroni and
cheese. I think the shock of having to digest
actual home-cooked food was too much for it. It
made a horrible gasping sound like a hippo being
suffocated and died a hideous death. Sadly, it had
a touch of drama queen and cannoned a fountain of
half-garbage-disposed roast beef about three feet
in the air.

Connor thought it was pretty cool. I think he
learned a new word when Mommy was cleaning roast
beef off the walls, though, so we will certainly
hear about it from his preschool teacher. (Rhymes
with snit; Connor said it 47 times before bedtime.)

You'll be glad to know that the plumber actually fixed it (the garbage disposal, not the bad
word thing) without having to install a new one.
In fact, according to Mom, he was a very nice and
cheerful man who turned some latch under the sink,
cleaned everything out, and was gone in less than
six minutes. For only $98.00. (Snit.)

No wonder he was cheerful. That's $980 per
hour. Our kids are definitely skipping college and
going straight to plumbing school. I bought Connor
a toy tool belt so he can start practicing now.

(By the way, I got your e-mail about care and
treatment of the septic tank. If you think for one

## E-mail to the Front

minute I am having *anything* to do with a septic
tank, the desert heat has melted your brain. Don't
ever, ever bring it up again.)

Anyway, back to Stephen King. Remember his
story about the industrial washing machine that
came to life and ate people in disgusting ways?
Well, I think our washing machine has been reading
my books and getting ideas, because tonight it
started making a horrible banging noise, like WHOMP
WHOMP WHOMP. I went running down to the basement
to see what was going on and *it had moved.* I am
not kidding. The washing machine was literally
about 10 feet across the basement floor from where
it was supposed to be, trailing tubes and cords
and whatnot. The floor was covered with water.

It was trying to make a break for it—I know it.
No longer content to eat one sock out of every
pair I put in it, it was coming upstairs to go
directly to the closet and bypass the middleman.

I was afraid to walk in the water, in case I got
electrocuted—you know how I am about electricity—
so I got your fishing waders and the broom and
advanced to the cord, to pull it out of the wall.
(I had your work-in-the-yard gloves on, too.)

Frankly, I was scared to death.

So there I was, in red flannel pajamas, rubber
hip waders, and huge leather gloves, brandishing a
broom. I pulled the plug with the end of the broom
and ran out of the room. I'll have to clean the
water up tomorrow, in the daylight.

There's no way I'm going back down there tonight.

Unfortunately, Connor had come downstairs during all this. He took one look at me and started laughing so hard he forgot he was potty trained. (Did I mention the carpet cleaning guys are coming Thursday?)

At this rate, it's going to be candlelight and beating our clothes on a rock to wash them, if you don't get back soon.

I'm almost afraid to write this to you, because I don't want the computer to tell the other appliances what's going on. They know when you fear them. They can smell it.

I'm not going near the toaster until you come home.

# Chapter 13

## *Staying Fit in Thirty Minutes a Month*

**July 2000**

**To:** Judd
**From:** Alesia
**Subject:** Exercise and other wishful thinking

I got your e-mail asking me why I'm planning to join the Y, when I have exercise videos, a treadmill, and a stationary bike at home. The easiest way to answer that is to describe my attempt to exercise yesterday. (Please keep in mind that my Mom is here to help for a few weeks now, so it may be even more interesting when she goes home.) Here are the highlights:

I spend two hours playing outside with Connor. When he's completely worn out, I say: "Mommy wants to do her exercise tape now."

Connor: "I'll help, Mommy." Runs to get weights. Drops 5-lb. dumbbell on my bare foot. Much hopping on one foot and loud noises.

I finally force the shoe on my swollen foot, as it turns black and purple, and insert the exercise tape into the VCR.

Enter my helpful mother, with a look of disgust on her face: "What are you doing? I'd go crazy if I had to do that kind of thing!"

I start abdominal exercises.

Connor puts his hand on my stomach and leans close, pressing all 32 pounds of his body weight into what *must* be a vital organ: "You're not doing it right, Mommy."

After much pleading with him to move back, I still almost hit Connor in the face with my elbow on the way up into the third abdominal crunch; his head is two inches from mine. "You need help, Mommy."

I begin arm exercises. Repeated warnings: "Stay back from Mommy." Almost hit Connor in the head with dumbbells, as he tries to Velcro himself to my exercise clothes.

Steroid-laden instructor on video begins one-armed triceps push-ups. I lack pharmaceutical enhancements; do two-armed push-ups. Connor and my mother both exclaim: "You're not doing it right."

My helpful mother adds: "Of course, that instructor weighs *much* less than you do."

She leaves the room. Reenters room with bowl of potato chips. Sounds of much crunching.

Lauren begins howling. I pause the VCR and stop to get her bottle. My Mom tries to give Lauren her bottle and becomes frustrated after many sincere attempts lasting a total of three seconds. I take baby, stop tape, nurse baby.

Lauren in crib, sleeping.

Connor ejects exercise tape, inserts Barney tape, throws astonishing fit at being asked to reverse process. Connor banished to bedroom television with tape of annoying purple dinosaur.

I begin exercise tape again.

Mom leaves room; reenters with bowl of pistachio nuts. Sounds of much shell cracking and crunching.

I learn my abs of steel have turned into abs of marshmallow sometime during the past three years and two babies.

30-minute tape finally ends, only two hours and 45 minutes later. I do cool-down stretches. My helpful mother leaves room; reenters with pan: "Would you like a brownie?"

Triumphant and unvanquished, I rush to weigh myself. Have gained a pound.

The problem with exercise and deployment is one of basic unfairness. Our spouses are actually getting paid to maintain good health and physical fitness. They're encouraged to work out daily. They even have periodic fun and fitness days, where they get to run a few miles on the beach in their stylish boots and fit in as many push-ups and sit-ups as they want.

This is sometimes called boot camp.

What's more, military exercise facilities boast first-class equipment and all the amenities. And it's free. It's sort of how I imagine Julia Roberts's life, except without the facials.

We spouses, however, are home trying to find thirty minutes a few times a week to keep our muscles from atrophying into Jell-O. We do have options, though. We can join a health club and pay $40 a month for the privilege of watching people with more time, more money, and better bodies hog the StairMaster.

Or we can try to find somebody to watch the kids while we take advantage of the free facility at the base. This has its own special reward—the privilege of being the only out-of-shape person in the gym at any given moment.

I have gone to the base gym at 5 A.M., 10 A.M., 3 P.M., and 10 P.M. I have tried to sneak in behind the janitor as he closed up. I have sacrificed coffee to get there before dawn. It doesn't matter when I go, there will be an announcement over the loudspeaker: "Warning! Warning! Chubby woman walking!"

When I finally get up the nerve to start exercising post-pregnancy, I find myself in line for the treadmill behind a team of Navy SEALs who just got done with a little light warm-up, like carrying a submarine across Oregon. On the surface, we have so much in common. Their muscles bulge, my belly bulges. Their abs are ripped, my T-shirt is ripped. Except for the faint aroma of regurgitated breast milk, nobody would ever guess I'm not one of them.

So, back in the real world, I lurk behind the free weights, trying to look like somebody who's going to bench press three hundred pounds any minute. Then I wait for the SEAL to finish running six-minute miles, so I can do my twenty minutes of power walking at a brisk twenty-seven-minute-per-mile pace.

Meanwhile, I try to blend in with a lot of sweaty guys who could bench-press my car. (Not that there's much of a downside to watching muscular guys do power squats.)

Finally, there's option three, otherwise known as reality. We do videos at 5 A.M. before the kids are up, during naptime, or at 11 P.M. after everyone is in bed. We Tae Bo, Tai Chi, and tie our bodies up in knots, because we're going to lose fifty pounds and look like a cross between Cameron Diaz and Angelina Jolie (except without the tattoo thing) by the time he gets back from deployment, by God. That lasts for about three weeks, and then we hit the wall that all serious athletes face: sleep deprivation and serious lack of interest. So, we alter our reality a little bit.

OK, we lie like a rug.

If I did nearly as much exercise as I claimed to be doing during deployment, I could run the Boston Marathon in thirty-nine minutes and play a few sets of tennis against the Williams sisters afterward to cool down.

Both of them. At the same time.

The happy news is that our spouses probably aren't doing much more exercise than chasing beers and running up tabs, because they're out being guys who miss their families and don't know what to do with themselves. So, let's face it, we'll all look the same at reunion, anyway.

# Chapter 14

## *Geography and Friendships: Relocation, Relocation, Relocation*

**To:** Judd
**From:** Alesia
**Subject:** I lost another friend today.

This has to be a new record. Only a few months after we moved from Florida to Washington, and I've already lost my first friend. Connor's godmother, no less. I have called and called and e-mailed and e-mailed—nothing. When I finally reached her, it was the same old story, "Oh, I've been busy."

I know we lose friends every time we move, but I've never had one I considered such a close friend drop off so fast before. It really hurts. So I've been pretty sad and melancholy, today. Friends are so precious and important; it really hurts to lose one.

I've been thinking about the geography/friendship thing. With five-cents-a-minute phone calls, and e-mail—which is *free*—you wouldn't think distance on a map would be so hard on relationships. But every time we move, we lose more friends. Of my four closest friends from law school in Columbus, only Andy stays in touch.

## E-mail to the Front

In fact, from 15 years of living in Columbus, I can count on the fingers of one hand the friends I still have. That's kind of pathetic. Even my maid of honor from our wedding never calls me. Whenever I call her, whether it has been four weeks or four months since we last talked, she always says, "Oh, I was *just* going to call you."

Right.

When we left Florida for here, same thing. I have high hopes for a few, though. Karen, Virginia, and Kelly all call and write.

The great thing about the Navy, at least, is that even though we have to move so much, we take some of our friends with us! Malia and Jason moved here before us, so I actually knew somebody. And I'm meeting lots of wonderful new friends through the spouse's club.

Still, it gets harder to keep trying to make friends, when you wonder how long they'll last.

I'm sorry I'm so melancholy today. I miss you so much and am feeling kind of lonely and abandoned. I'll try to cheer up and write more later.

Military life can be very isolating in one way and very community-oriented in another. I've never been in such a close group that supports each other as well as squadron families do. The spouses welcome you warmly, invite you into existing friendships, and share their experiences and advice. They bring meals to families with new babies and flowers to those facing sickness or death. They organize over-the-hump parties, weekly coffees, get-togethers for the kids, and social gatherings. You never have to be alone, if you take the opportunity to become involved.

The isolation comes into play in your friendships with civilians. Sometimes it's hard to explain what you're going through, without feeling like you're whining. It's rough trying to make close friends at work, when you know you may be moving to the other side of the country or halfway around the world in a matter of months. It's inevitable that many of these friendships will fall by the wayside, victims of geography and busy lives.

Before Judd's second deployment, we moved to a city halfway between north Whidbey Island (where Judd works when he's not on deployment) and Seattle (where I work). We each face about a three-hour round-trip commute daily. Mine is sometimes a little less, if traffic is light. In Seattle, it almost never is.

While it was great to be able to work in my field, which I couldn't do on Whidbey, and I found good friends among my new colleagues, I missed out on the social camaraderie of the squadron spouses, due to the distance. I missed a lot. Nothing is quite the same as being able to talk to people who *understand,* because they're going through the same thing.

It's a feeling of relief seeping through your bones, as if your very body relaxes into the warmth of acceptance and understanding. I don't have to explain why a late homecoming—an extra nineteen days on top of six months—is such a very big deal. I don't have to hear: "My husband knows better than to call *me* at 4 A.M."

For me, it's a split-personality existence sometimes. I have wonderful friends in the military community, and I have amazing friends in my civilian life. It's just that I don't usually see them both at the same gatherings.

And I've had to come to terms with leaving some of them behind when we move. It always hurts. But true friendships transcend distance.

Thank goodness for e-mail.

# Chapter 15

## Military Spouses' Clubs: Sharing Tears, Laughter . . . and Quilt Squares?

August 2000

**To:** Judd
**From:** Alesia
**Subject:** Recipe cards and other foreign concepts

I keep getting reminders from the OSC that they need my quilt square and recipe card.

They must be kidding.

I feel a little like I've time-traveled back to the 1950s here. I've never known anyone in my entire life who quilts or trades recipe cards. It wasn't really part of the curriculum in law school: "Yes, Miss Holliday, please analyze the First Amendment and present your recipe for chicken casserole."

But, when in Rome . . . So I thought I'd give it a shot. The problem is, I've never even walked into a fabric store in my adult life. I have a vague memory of going with Mom once when I was a kid, but she made that hideous three-piece suit out of red-and-white-checked fabric that I had to wear to school, and I looked like a red-haired tablecloth. The whole thing was pretty traumatic.

I've never been back.

## E-mail to the Front

So, anyway, the fabric store. You don't buy fabric by the inch or the foot or any normal measurement; it's something like by the bolt, or by the hectare. I'd probably wind up buying enough material to slipcover your plane, because I'd be too embarrassed to admit I didn't know one bolt equals six miles in fabric terms.

Then what?? I have those antique quilts, and they're sewn in beautiful hand-stitching. Do I have to go buy sewing needles and thread, too? There's a WHOLE AISLE of different kinds of needles.

And recipe cards. I *know* you're cracking up over that one. The last time I got creative in the kitchen, it was to see if Strawberry Pop-Tarts really do catch on fire in the toaster, like Dave Barry said. (They do.)

Do you think if I bought some chocolate chips, cut the recipe off the back of the package, and glued it on the card, it would be OK? I've never actually baked them, but they must be good if it's on the package, right?

I can't believe I'm getting an inferiority complex over quilt squares. I really need to get a job.

I really need to get a life.

**To:** Alesia
**From:** Judd
**Subject:** You promised not to set the kitchen on fire again.

Please—no more Pop-Tart experiments. We talked about that. And remember to cook everything on LOW HEAT.

AND remember: I put the fire extinguisher on top of the refrigerator before I left.

**To:** Judd
**From:** Alesia
**Subject:** New friends

I don't know why I was so worried about the whole quilt thing. I went to a meeting of the OSC, and everyone was wonderful! So kind and gracious, and willing to share tips for how to manage six months of deployment. (There are other people who don't know how to quilt, either, so I didn't feel like a *total* buffoon.)

p.s. I am *not* going to set the kitchen on fire again. I can't believe you bring up every teeny mistake. You put the flames out right away, anyway.

(I made up a list of instructions for the fire extinguisher in big, bold type and taped it on the fridge, just in case.)

The spouses' clubs are a wonderful source of support and cama-raderie all the time, but especially during deployment. Like any social organization, the groups are a reflection of their members. The OSC for Judd's squadron on Whidbey had the advantage of having caring people (who were amazingly organized) running it. So, there were planned activities all throughout deployment; gatherings for the kids, over-the-hump parties, and many informal activities that made sure you never had to be alone for long, if you didn't want to be.

Carrie, Robin, Dawn, and Margo were just a few of many won-derful people I met through the OSC, and I really enjoyed the events that the kids and I attended.

In spite of that unhealthy obsession with quilt squares.

# Chapter 16

## *Phone Calls at 4 A.M.*

**To:** Judd
**From:** Alesia
**Subject:** I'm so glad you called.

I told you it doesn't matter if it's 4 a.m. here when you get a chance to get to a phone. I'd much rather have you wake me up than not hear from you at all. It has been a week and a half since your last phone call. Almost two weeks since your last e-mail. Please don't waste a single second of our time to talk saying you're sorry for waking me up! I miss you so much!

**To:** Alesia
**From:** Judd
**Subject:** I miss you too!

I felt bad for waking you up. I know sleep is a precious commodity there! But I was so glad to talk to you. I hope the boxes of presents start arriving soon. I know you will like the clock! I'll talk to you tomorrow. Hopefully I'll be able to figure out the computer modem thing, which will allow me to call you on the computer without being cut off any moment.

**To:** Judd
**From:** Alesia
**Subject:** I can't be held responsible for what I say
in my sleep.

And "it must be 4 a.m." is *not* grouchy. Not
really. Not in a mean way. You do have an amazing
capacity for calling me in the middle of the
night, you have to admit. It was just one of those
growth-spurt nights where Lauren refused to sleep
and kept waking up, so when I finally fell asleep
at 3 a.m. I felt like I was dying.

So I was a teeny bit crabby when you called. But,
once I woke up, I was delighted that you finally
were near a phone!! Unfortunately, you hung up
about 20 minutes before I really woke up. Sorry.

A thirteen- to seventeen-hour-time difference is tough. When
Judd got up to fly at the crack of dawn, we were already in bed for the
night. By the time he got back from flying, we were running errands
or at the park. Sometimes we had to compromise and talk at 4 A.M.

OK. Lots of times.

But it was better to talk in the middle of the night than not at all.
E-mail is wonderful. Cards and letters are cherished. But the sound
of his voice was the real connection. When I heard his voice, I could
see his smile. When I heard his laugh, I could smell his aftershave.
When he said he loved me, I could feel his arms around me in the
hug I needed so much. All of that just from the sound of his voice.

I could always catch up on sleep *after* deployment.

# Chapter 17

## *That's Classified*

August 2000

**To:** Judd
**From:** Alesia
**Subject:** Hello, wherever you are and whatever you're doing

It's a little frustrating not knowing where you are, what you're doing, or when you might be able to call. I know you're not getting e-mails all that often, either, since you usually respond to a week's worth in one two-paragraph response. This takes "husband-wife communication problems" to a whole new level. I think I should go on *Oprah* on a segment titled "You Think Your Husband Doesn't Talk To YOU? HA." When we do talk, it's not like you can tell me anything, anyway. Which I do understand, by the way (Loose Lips Sink Ships and all that), but that doesn't make it any easier.

## E-mail to the Front

**To:** Alesia
**From:** Judd
**Subject:** Communications

I have been trying to log onto the AOL mail account, but the server here keeps kicking me off. I know it's tough not to hear from me, but I'm really doing the best I can. We just don't get anywhere near a phone or computer very often, and when we do, there are 50 guys in line for the phone, so I try to keep it short so everybody gets a chance to call home. It's not like our cell phone works on Middle Eastern calling networks. Not that we'd necessarily be allowed to use it, anyway.

This has been a long, hot day. We had FOD walkdown this morning (cleaning Foreign Objects and Debris off the runway). Then the plane washing took about three hours, and the temperature got up to 126F. It's not something that I want to do again soon! I got back from the airfield a little while ago, and am doing laundry, getting a haircut, and e-mailing you. How did the lawn mower thing turn out?

I can't really say where we are, but we are getting ready to leave tomorrow and go someplace else for a few weeks. At some point, we will be in Diego Garcia, and I'll try to call you from there. Bear with me; when I get home, I'll talk to you nonstop for three days straight, until you're tired of hearing from me! I feel like I have been away a lifetime. I miss you all so much.

**To:** Judd
**From:** Alesia
**Subject:** I hate not knowing where you are.

But I know, I know. Don't ask.

We had a terrific day today; went to the park and to the library for story hour. I even took a nap when the kids did! Talk about bliss! I hope you're OK.

**To:** Alesia
**From:** Judd
**Subject:** Patience is a virtue.

I still can't tell you where I am, please don't ask. Just be assured that I am somewhere very safe! I'll try and call you when I can.

**To:** Judd
**From:** Alesia
**Subject:** I *wasn't* asking.

And, of course, you *always* have to keep "very safe" places secret.

Be careful.

**To:** Alesia
**From:** Judd
**Subject:** We have a great crew.

Hello, sweetie. I'm sorry I'm only able to contact you intermittently. I am fine and you shouldn't worry. I got some good news this evening that most of the crew (the enlisted guys) are getting awards for the work that they've been doing over the last few months. I can't go into the details of course, but these guys have really made a difference in things. I will spend the day writing the awards out for the crew, so please send all of your creative writing thoughts my way. I'll try to call you this evening but, if not, I'll call you when I get to the next place.

**To:** Judd
**From:** Alesia
**Subject:** The Next Place

I get it. This is back to that It's Not Just a Marriage, It's an Adventure thing, isn't it? Please stay safe—wherever you are and wherever you're going—and remember my crucial aircraft advice: Always land as many times as you take off.

Judd is what's known as a "mustang" in military terminology—an officer who was previously enlisted. He enlisted when he was just a teenager and served for several years on submarines, before he went to college and then was commissioned as an officer. When he graduated, he had the opportunity to go back on subs. He wanted to fly this time, though, and I agreed wholeheartedly. The life of a submariner's wife is pretty tough. Submarines can go under for weeks at a time (don't ask how deep, I already tried. That's Classified), and there is no contact at all with home during that time. No phone calls, no e-mail, no nothing.

Sub guys' wives deserve special awards for courage and patience.

Then there are Special Forces. SEALs, Delta Force, and the rest of the combat units ready to go in at any time, at a word. There's no planning or warning. If you're married to a SEAL, he can get the call in the middle of your anniversary dinner, your child's birthday party, or your vacation, and he'll have to be wheels up in a matter of hours. You don't know where he's going or how long he'll be gone. You just know he'll be on the front line in a very scary place. They don't get a lot of chances to call home, either.

Special Forces's spouses are on my heroes list, too.

But, as hard as it is for all of us to go days or weeks with no word, I think about how much more painful and frightening it must have been to be a military spouse in the old days, when there was no e-mail or cell phones. When CNN didn't report on every movement. When it took weeks or months for some families to hear if their loved ones had survived Pearl Harbor.

I would rather not know where Judd is, if silence keeps our military forces safe. I would rather not hear about troop movements on the news, if discretion keeps even one soldier or sailor alive.

## E-mail to the Front

Everyone asks how we can possibly live with not knowing. It's simple. We don't have any choice. So we wait and wonder, pray, and e-mail. Sometimes we cry.

And we're overjoyed to get phone calls at 4 A.M. from our spouses. From wherever.

# Chapter 18

## *Is It Safe to Eat Month-Old Cookies?*

**August 2000**

**To:** Judd
**From:** Alesia
**Subject:** Just call me Betty Crockpot.

We made homemade cookies today and mailed them to you. I don't understand why you want these, considering you move around so much that the mail may take weeks to catch up. Is it safe to eat month-old cookies?

I guess, with my cooking, a better question would be whether they're safe to eat fresh out of the oven. Connor was very suspicious of cookies that didn't come from a package, but I finally got him to taste one. He pronounced it *almost* as good as the kind we slice and bake.

By the way, please let me know if/when you get my boxes. Do you appreciate them? Do you even notice what's in them? You never say much about them.

**To:** Alesia
**From:** Judd
**Subject:** HELLO!!! IS THIS THING ON???

So I find it difficult to talk with my mouth full! Yes, I appreciate and love the boxes you send me! They are GIFTS FROM HEAVEN, MANNA FOR THE SOUL, FOOD FOR THE CREW. I ADORE YOU.

Things are not as advertised here. The "great AOL access" no longer exists. There are only two phone lines into this place for us. One goes into the office, the other to a phone in the middle of the area where we live called the "Wadi." It is much cooler here, but much more windy. The wind is always blowing about 15 mph and usually gusts up higher to about 25-30 mph.

To send e-mail here, you have to use the official address I gave you and put my name in the subject line. If you don't put my name on the subject line, I won't get it, since they sort the e-mail that comes into the one computer that does e-mail by subject.

There is absolutely nothing to do but study, eat, exercise, and fly. Which is probably good, because that's all we have time to do.

I got another box today. Yaay!! More stuff!! I love getting stuff (especially because it makes everyone else jealous of my beautiful wife and above-average, superintelligent, and amazing children).

Thank you again for sending all those wonderful things. I shared the chocolate-chip cookies with the crew during our flight tonight. They were VERY appreciated! I'm saving all the brownies for myself, though. The boxes have never taken longer than a couple of weeks to get here, so the cookies are sometimes a little bit stale, but still great!

Trust me, with some of the unfamiliar foods I've been eating, stale cookies are the least of my worries. Thanks for the Tums.

In our squadron, we have a tradition called "Adopt the Single Sailors." This means that we divide up the men and women who aren't married and "adopt" them for purposes of sending them care packages during the deployments.

I always felt sorry for the guys who got me.

It's not that I didn't try. I bought little gifts and sent lots of food. Food that I didn't actually cook, preferably. It was better for everybody that way.

The problem is that the crews move around so much. It's not like the different flight crews in a squadron are in the same place at the same time. It may take quite a while for a package to catch up to its intended recipient. You don't want to send chocolate, for example. But receiving a box of (nonperishable) goodies from home can make a big difference in morale. We kept "Daddy's box" in the corner of the kitchen and filled it up with treats, the kids' artwork, magazines, mail, and love as the week went by. When it filled up (about once every week or ten days), we shipped it out and started the next one.

## E-mail to the Front

Sometimes the cookies were too stale to eat by the time they reached Judd, or they were crumpled into tiny bits from rough handling of the box. He didn't care. He was just glad to know we were thinking of him.

It was the chocolate-chip equivalent of hugs.

# Chapter 19

## *Over the Hump*

**To:** Judd
**From:** Alesia
**Subject:** We're halfway there!

And please let it be spring soon! I think we are all going to go insane if we're stuck indoors because of the rain much longer. I was literally ready to hang the children upside down by their toenails. But WE'RE HALFWAY THERE!! Now, it's all downhill!

**To:** Judd
**From:** Alesia
**Subject:** Only halfway there

It occurred to me this morning that we still have three months to go. Three long months. You know, the Prowler squadrons only have three-month deployments. Is it too late to change sides? To be fair, they *do* have to go out every six months, so you're all gone the same ridiculous amount of time.

**To:** Alesia
**From:** Judd
**Subject:** Over the hump

Did you go to the over-the-hump party? Did you have fun? Did you pick up the lawn mower attachments? Have to get some sleep; flying tomorrow. We're halfway there!! Just a few short weeks until we come home. I'm at the library and the kind person behind the desk has informed me that I have 5 more minutes, which I find VERY annoying. Five minutes is not nearly enough time to tell you how much I love and miss you and Connor and Lauren.

**To:** Judd
**From:** Alesia
**Subject:** What is this unnatural obsession you have with the lawn mower?

It's past mowing season, anyway. We went to the park yesterday and walked around the lake, and Lauren practiced sitting up on the blanket. Then we came home and had a "picnic" in the living room and played more, and I read the ENTIRE 92-page Disney book to Connor (over an hour and a half, even with my much-abbreviated version of the stories; nobody dies or loses any parents in *my* world). Then bath for everyone and finally bed.

Take care. Your lovely wife, whom you adore, and who is now going to go get the LAWN MOWER ATTACHMENTS.

p.s. Did I mention I can't wait till you're home, and I will never bathe another child for at least a year? That can be *Daddy's* job (along with the mowing, the car-to-the-shop trips, the fix-computer-stuff jobs, the grocery shopping, the cleaning . . .), oh, sorry, where was I? Oh, right, on my way to the store for the LAWN MOWER ATTACH-MENTS. Don't think I didn't notice that you won't be home till December, and there won't be any more mowing going on, then.

Over the Hump. Halfway there. At the halfway point, I first started to believe I could make it. After all, we only had to get through another chunk of time the same size as the one we'd just managed. The middle of deployment is the easiest, I think. The first weeks are a flurry of getting everyone's routine restructured into life without one parent; without your spouse. The anguish of freshly minted loneliness.

The final weeks before homecoming are filled with anxiety about seeing him again; the stress of trying to get everything done before he gets back. Those last weeks last forever.

But the time in between is like the middle trimester of a pregnancy. You've settled in for the long haul, and know you can make it. The early pains and nausea have subsided, and you've come to terms with the changes in your life and routine. You can even eat again! It's smooth sailing on calm seas. And the exact middle point—over the hump—buoys you with the excitement of knowing the hardest part is over.

Halfway there. I can do this. *We* can do this.

Ninety-one more paper chain links to go.

# Chapter 20

## Chasing Children, Running After Raccoons, and Other Aerobic Exercise

October 2000

**To:** Judd
**From:** Alesia
**Subject:** Where do they get all that energy?

I am worn out. We went to a fall harvest party the squadron held down at the pumpkin patch. There was a big corn maze (I kept saying a "maize maze" and getting strange looks; nobody thinks I'm funny) and we hiked all through it. I wonder who had that brilliant idea—"Hey, let's mow some paths in the cornfield and get a bunch of dumb city folks to pay us $5 to walk through it!" Sheer genius. The farmers must be laughing all the way to the bank, as they say.

We bought pumpkins to carve and had ice cream. Lauren was in baby heaven; she went after my ice cream cone with the face-first method. Not really efficient, but she was ecstatic about her first ice cream.

I thought they'd be worn out, but no such luck. We are watching the new *Toy Story* video. "Buzz, I AM your father!" I was cracking up, and Connor looked at me like I was nuts. (The kid just

doesn't get *Star Wars* references.) Lauren climbed
all over me and drooled. She thinks I'm her personal teething ring. I had to clean up the bird
poop in the house, but I think the raccoon scared
the bird away.

**To:** Alesia
**From:** Judd
**Subject:** WHAT raccoon? BIRD POOP???

You drive me nuts. What raccoon? How did a bird
get in the house? What are you talking about??? I
will call you as soon as we get back from flying.
Deer, dog-eating coyotes, birds, and raccoons.
Unbelievable.

**To:** Judd
**From:** Alesia
**Subject:** Miscellaneous wildlife

Sorry I ended that last e-mail so abruptly; had
to go get the baby. You know the mail slot in the
wall (next to the door) that doesn't close? A bird
apparently got into the house through there. (There
were a couple of feathers caught in it.) But he
must have gotten out the same way, because there
was bird poop on the floor but no bird. The bigger
surprise was when P.J. went nuts when we got home,
barking like a wild dog. He zoomed into the bedroom and was just freaking out. I followed him in
there, and he had a raccoon "treed" on the dresser.

After closing the dog and the kids in the bathroom, I got the broom and "encouraged" Rocky Raccoon to leave. We can't figure out how he got in, which is not very reassuring. One more Close Encounter of the Animal Kind, and I am moving to the city.

Any city.

**To:** Judd
**From:** Alesia
**Subject:** busy day; no raccoons

We played Indy 500 with the stroller and tricycle today. Connor careened around and around your truck, and I chased him with the stroller. Lauren was squealing with baby joy. Mommy was panting with postnatal exercise-avoidance distress. It was good for all of us. Connor got very upset when I caught him; I was only supposed to pursue him and never catch up, apparently. (He also gets ticked off when he loses at Candy Land. It's not my fault I always get Queen Frostine; you have to play these games to *win*.)

He must get this unpleasant competitive streak from you. He cheats at Chutes and Ladders, too.

p.s. There is a package on its way to you. I found the dress medals you need and wrapped them in some of your underwear for padding, so don't open the box in front of everyone or you might get teased a bit. After the whole nipple thing, I don't want to make *that* mistake again.

# Chapter 21

## *ThreatCon Delta*

October 18, 2000

**To:** Judd
**From:** Alesia
**Subject:** ThreatCon Delta for Bahrain

I saw on the news that U.S. Central Command officials have declared Threat Condition Delta, the highest threat level, in Bahrain and Qatar. I know we went to ThreatCon Charlie immediately after the attack on the *Cole*. Evidently the latest recent threat assessment forced the Pentagon to raise the threat level in Bahrain "where about 1,100 U.S. service members are stationed, and in Qatar, where fewer than 50 U.S. service members tend pre-positioned equipment," according to the DOD website. In other words, precisely where you are.

I need to go find out exactly what ThreatCon Delta means. My shorthand version has always been: ThreatCon Alpha: Mildly scary; ThreatCon Bravo: Moderately scary; ThreatCon Charlie: Extremely scary; and ThreatCon Delta: Completely terrifying.

I know there are more technical definitions, but I'm betting that they add up to the same thing. I love you, and I am completely terrified. Please be safe.

## E-mail to the Front

**The Terrorist Threat Conditions, as defined on the DOD website:**

A Chairman of the Joint Chiefs of Staff–approved program standardizes the military services' identification of, and recommended responses to, terrorist threats against U.S. personnel and facilities. This program facilitates interservice coordination and support for antiterrorism activities. Also called ThreatCons. There are four ThreatCons above normal:

### ThreatCon Alpha

This condition applies when there is a general threat of possible terrorist activity against personnel and facilities, the nature and extent of which are unpredictable, and circumstances do not justify full implementation of ThreatCon Bravo measures. However, it may be necessary to implement certain measures from higher ThreatCons resulting from intelligence received or as a deterrent. The measures in this ThreatCon must be capable of being maintained indefinitely.

### ThreatCon Bravo

This condition applies when an increased and more predictable threat of terrorist activity exists. The measures in this ThreatCon must be capable of being maintained for weeks without causing undue hardship, affecting operational capability, and aggravating relations with local authorities.

### ThreatCon Charlie

This condition applies when an incident occurs, or intelligence is received, indicating some form of terrorist action against personnel and facilities is imminent. Implementation of measures in this ThreatCon for more than a short period probably will create hardship and affect the peacetime activities of the unit and its personnel.

*ThreatCon Delta*

This condition applies in the immediate area where a terrorist attack has occurred or when intelligence has been received that terrorist action against a specific location or person is likely. Normally, this ThreatCon is declared as a localized condition. See also antiterrorism.

I still like my definitions better.

# Chapter 22

## *When Bad Things Happen*

On October 12, 2000, at around noon in the Persian Gulf, terrorists bombed the USS Cole as she refueled in Aden, Yemen. Seventeen sailors died and many more were injured. Nobody knew who or what would be the next target. Judd's squadron was based in Bahrain and right in the line of fire. Credible threats were made against U.S. forces in the region.

**October 12**

**To:** Judd
**From:** Alesia
**Subject:** Are you OK? I can't believe this!

The news keeps changing—first they said four sailors died; then maybe 12, and now they're just not sure. Where are you? Are you safe? I keep crying for those poor families wondering if their son or daughter, husband or wife, or Mommy or Daddy is among the dead. What if they try to bomb the base where you are? Please get in touch with me as soon as you can. We are all going insane.

October 14

**To:** Alesia
**From:** Judd
**Subject:** We're OK.

Sorry not to have written sooner. We have been a little busy lately. On our way to Qatar, everything broke loose, and we ended up helping to evacuate people. We had other planes taking investigators and medical personnel to Yemen. Our crew ended up in the Sheraton Downtown with orders to pretty much stay in the room and wait for the phone to ring. We flew a regular mission today, and have the Ready tomorrow, when we will move back into the barracks. We're pretty tired, but working on. We are all fine, although I miss you very, very much. I'll try and call you once we get moved back into the barracks tomorrow. I love and miss you all VERY VERY much.

October 22

**To:** VP-40 Marlin Families
**From:** Carrie Ryan
**Subject:** Important news from Commander Ryan

Dear Marlin Families:

CDR Ryan just called this morning and wanted me to pass on the following information to you:

- They are taking all our guys out of Bahrain today and moving them to Diego Garcia. There has been no threat to our guys but they are doing it for precautionary measures.

- Everyone is fine.

- We do not know how long they will stay there at this time.

- Everyone in Masirah is fine and will stay there on the military base.

That is all the information I have at this time. We'll keep you posted if we hear of any news.

**October 22, later**

**To:** VP-40 Marlin Families
**From:** CDR Ryan
**Subject:** Update

To our Marlin Families:

Here is an update on our Bahrain detachment:
Last night we got word that there was some concern about the security of our P-3s in Bahrain. The Vice Admiral who is in charge of the Navy for the Persian Gulf, VADM Moore, felt it would be best to move our planes back to Diego Garcia until he could assess the situation better. I want to make it clear that there was no threat made to our people or our aircraft; this was purely precautionary.
Since we were given the direction to move the planes, I decided to move a number of people that are detached there. Our 3 planes have left Bahrain,

two are in Diego Garcia and one is in Muscat, Oman. Our one plane went to Muscat because it had an in-flight emergency and had to divert there. Everyone is OK and the crew did a great job handling the emergency. The plane is being fixed and should be on its way to Diego Garcia tomorrow.

I want to make it clear that there was no threat to our people in Bahrain. The families that are permanently stationed there, many live out in town, are still carrying on with life as they have for the last several weeks. The local school is still in session. I kept 19 people behind in Bahrain to prepare for our return and assist the Admiral's staff with our operations. All 19 are living on base. Attached is a list of people that stayed behind.

I hope this helps clear up the picture of what is going on over here. I am sure you have a lot of questions and it must be frustrating being so far away and hungry for information. Please don't hesitate to contact me. I will try to keep you informed as I get more information.

Sincerely, CDR Bernie Ryan

**To:** Judd
**From:** Alesia
**Subject:** I am so worried about you

I had a horrible dream that you were dead. It upset me so much that I kept waking up, and every time I fell back asleep, I had the same dream.

It was your crew that had the emergency, wasn't it? You really have to call me at the earliest opportunity, or I am going to lose my mind.

I got a message from CDR Ryan that you are being evac'd to Diego, so at least you'll be able to call me from there. We are all praying for you and for everyone on the *Cole* and their families.

**October 24**

**To:** VP-40 Marlin Families
**From:** CDR Ryan
**Subject:** Update for 24 Oct.

To all Fighting Marlin Families:

I can only imagine the questions you must have about what is going on over here. First, I want to say that everyone is fine and doing a fantastic job under some very challenging circumstances. As many of you know, two nights ago, we were told to evacuate our P-3s located in Bahrain. Bahrain was put on a heightened alert, and Admiral Moore felt it was best to move some of his assets away, ships and planes, until this passed.

Once we received this order, we immediately got our people together and flew the majority of them back to Diego Garcia on our 3 P-3s. As I mentioned on the previous note, CAC 6 diverted into Muscat, Oman, to take care of a malfunction on their aircraft. That aircraft and crew are still there and probably will be on their way to Diego Garcia within a day or two. The other two P-3s arrived here early yesterday morning.

We have 19 VP-40 Sailors in Bahrain who are there to assist the Admiral's staff and prepare for our eventual return. They are all confined to the base and well protected. I was in Bahrain just last week and I can assure you the Marines are fully alerted and doing a fantastic job protecting the base.

Last night VADM Moore, the Admiral in charge of our forces in Bahrain, had a "Town Meeting" with everyone stationed in Bahrain. He assured them there had been no threats to Americans.

I would like to address three issues that have come up in the news:

Threat Condition D or Delta: This condition must be set when a serious threat has been made to forces in the region. It is important to note that the Persian Gulf is a volatile area, but Bahrain is considered the most secure of all the locations. Also, this "region" includes a very large area which encompasses some historically dangerous locations, e.g., Syria, Iran, and Iraq.

Evacuation: There has been no evacuation or any plan to evacuate the people permanently stationed in Bahrain.

School Closure: Today Admiral Moore chose to close the school so they could conduct a thorough review of the security procedures in place there. In his "town hall" meeting last night, he discussed the school closing and was careful to try to reassure everyone that there has been no threat to the people there and in particular the school.

Life in Masirah has continued on without any interruptions. We continue to fly our scheduled flights there. They are also assisting with the repair of our P-3 in Muscat. Our crews in Diego Garcia are flying training flights and continuing on with deployment as planned. Two crews will be heading back to Thailand tomorrow and then on to Japan, so they can participate in a multinational exercise and hopefully get to track some submarines.

As you can see, we are continuing to operate. We have not been told when we might be able to go back to Bahrain and operate there. Until that time, we will continue to perform our missions in Diego Garcia and Masirah. Our people in Bahrain will continue to assist the Admiral's staff and keep us informed of the upcoming operations.

I will continue to keep you updated on the events over here. The only thing I can promise is that this is a constantly changing situation, and the stories you hear may conflict with some previous news you have been told. Many times the news reports comment on the region in general, and this is a very diverse region, so the report may not always apply to Bahrain or Masirah. Please be patient and trust that we will do our best to protect our incredible Fighting Marlin Sailors and at the same time keep you up to date with any changing news.

If you hear anything and are uncomfortable, please do not hesitate to send an e-mail to CDR

Clyde Porter (XO) or me or our hard-working Ombudsmen. We will be happy to answer any of your questions. I would feel much better knowing you are well informed, so please write. Our VP-40 families are my number one concern, whether it is you at home or our Sailors here.

You are always in our thoughts and prayers.

CDR Bernie Ryan, CO, VP-40 Fighting Marlins
"Laging Handa"—Always Ready

**To:** Judd
**From:** Alesia
**Subject:** I *knew* it was your crew.

Remember all those emergency procedures we kept practicing in Pensacola?? You better be safe or else.

October 25, a.m.

**To:** VP-40 Marlin Families
**From:** CDR Ryan
**Subject:** Update for 25 Oct.

To all Fighting Marlin Families and Friends:

I saw the news this morning (which is always one day old) and can see why there is such concern for our squadron members still in Bahrain.

I want to stress that the threats against Bahrain that have been mentioned in the press have been threats against U.S. assets, not people. This is why we flew out our planes. As I mentioned in the previous notes, the U.S. Navy ships were also sortied out of port. It is important to realize that the ship piers and airport are several miles away from the Naval Support Activity Bahrain, NSA Bahrain as it is commonly called, where our people are staying. NSA Bahrain has always been a very secure facility. The security forces have instituted additional measures and procedures in response to these threats, and we have restricted our people to on-base activities only. If it is felt that our people's safety is in doubt, we will immediately fly them out.

**October 25, p.m.**

**To:** VP-40 Marlin Families
**From:** CDR Ryan
**Subject:** Update for 25 Oct.

To all Fighting Marlin Families and Friends:

Life has started to settle down here. Nothing has changed in Bahrain, and that can be considered good news. In Masirah and Diego Garcia we have continued to perform all our missions and training events. I just got off the phone with the detachment in Bahrain, and they passed on that there has not been any developing news or changes to the threat condition. One interesting fact is that the airport is back open to a limited number of military logistics flights.

Again, please do not hesitate to contact me.
I will let you know as soon as I hear if anything
changes.
Warmest regards, CDR Bernie Ryan

**October 26**

**To:** Alesia
**From:** Judd
**Subject:** Finally in Diego

We got in last night around midnight, and I
spent most of the day here waiting to get some
money so that I could buy a phone card. I have
the phone card, and have reactivated my Internet
access here, so I am going to call. I'm sorry you
were so worried. The flight back from Muscat was
without incident, and entirely boring (which I
know you like!). There is talk they will be
reopening Bahrain for our planes in a week or so,
but no one is sure of course. I love you! I'll
talk to you in a few minutes!

**October 26**

**To:** All our friends and family
**From:** Alesia
**Subject:** Judd is finally safe in Diego Garcia.

He called this morning. They finally repaired
the airplane after the emergency landing in Oman,
in order to leave Oman for Diego. ThreatCon Delta
is still in effect in Bahrain. The few of the

## E-mail to the Front

squadron still in Bahrain are being heavily guarded by the Marines.

He said it was a boring flight!!! I told him boring was good, after recent events.

He has Internet access, so you can e-mail him yourself and say hi.

They may be returning to Bahrain as early as next week. I will keep you updated. Thanks again for your prayers and concern. They helped us so very much.

# Chapter 23

## Why Military Spouses Deserve Combat Pay

**To:** Judd
**From:** Alesia
**Subject:** My career is like a weird dance: One step forward, five steps back.

Moving from state to state, and having to start all over each time, is not really the greatest career path in my field. I just interviewed with that small firm on Whidbey. They were great; they loved me. Unfortunately, they offered me less money than I made my first year out of law school. I can't stand it.

And, THIS is fun—we just had an EARTHQUAKE!! I am officially freaked out. The whole house shook and my adrenaline shot through the roof. I'm watching the news, and it looks like the epicenter was clear down south of Seattle, so it wasn't too bad here. But there was some serious damage in Seattle and Tacoma. Wow! I thought I left earthquakes behind when we left Turkey.

Lauren is sick again and has been unable to sleep, because her poor baby nose is running like a faucet. I have her asleep in an upright position in her car seat now, so she can breathe. It took two hours of rocking to get her to sleep. I hope they both sleep through the night; I'm so tired I fell asleep on the floor in the middle of the Lincoln log forts Connor and I made this afternoon. (Getting poked in the eye by the fort flag woke me up pretty quick.)

I took the Explorer to have the last three recalled tires replaced (includes the spare). I feel much safer. I hadn't planned to have to do this today, but we picked up a nail in one so I just did the whole thing at once.

I had to secretly pack the Halloween decorations away today. Connor is vehemently opposed to my boxing them up and it's not worth the battle. I'm going to wait to do the Christmas decorating until you get home. Doesn't that sound wonderful: "until you get home." Only 30 more links or so!!!

Anyway, back to the job topic, I'm pretty sure I'm not going to take this job. It's not in my field, so I'd have the stress of learning a whole new area and getting paid a lot less. If I'm going to be away from my children, it needs to be worth it to me. I may need to look in Seattle. Let's talk about it when you get home.

Being a military spouse can be a tough sell to a prospective employer. Once you say: "I'll work really hard for the eighteen months to three years I'll be in this state," you're not really on the top of the hiring list. In my field, there were the added issues of having to take bar exams to get licensed in each different state. Which is about as much fun as poking yourself in the eye with a hot stick, only the hot stick thing wouldn't take three days and cost hundreds of dollars.

I've been pretty lucky, in that each time we moved, I found wonderful firms where I could work with, and learn from, talented people and do interesting work. But, it's not always easy. Living on Whidbey Island, for example, was very limiting. There's just not enough of a local economy to absorb hiring the spouses of all the personnel assigned to the base. Many spouses are, of course, stay-at-home Moms by choice, like I was for the first year of each of my children's lives. Some are stay-at-home Moms out of necessity, because the balance sheet doesn't work out to pay a baby-sitter more than your take-home pay.

Even some spouses who *don't* have children couldn't find jobs, or had to commute two to three hours per day to and from work. It's very tiring and adds to the overall stress in military families.

The bottom line about the men and women serving in the Armed Forces is that they have very little autonomy in their jobs. They can't call in sick randomly, or take a personal day without lots of advance notice and paperwork. They can't say, "Hey, I know we're flying an eleven-hour training mission today, but let's head down at noon so I can take a long lunch and go to my son's Thanksgiving Day pageant."

Not even if Connor gets to be the head Pilgrim.

So the spouse picks up the slack. All the slack. All the time. And this is another strain on their jobs. When you're the one who always has to stay home with the sick child, or to meet the plumber, or the cable guy, even the most understanding of bosses may get impatient. Some jobs have more flexibility than others. Some have rigid hours and days requirements, so one ear infection timed during a spouse's two-week detachment to parts unknown blows a year's worth of sick leave.

## E-mail to the Front

It's a Herculean juggling act, and it doesn't always work out right. Sometimes one of the balls smashes into the ground. And it can't be the "parent" ball, so it's always the "employee" ball. Sometimes I wish *we* earned combat pay, too. Or at least an extra few days' sick leave.

# Chapter 24

## *Loneliness and Cold Feet*

**To:** Judd
**From:** Alesia
**Subject:** You have been replaced by wool socks.

I solved the problem of ice-cold feet with wool socks and an electric blanket. It's been tough, not having your warm feet to put my cold ones on.

But all the socks in the world can't help with this crushing loneliness.

It's 3 a.m. (again, why am I always awake at 3 a.m.?), and there is a black space in my heart that won't go away.

You're my best friend. I miss being able to tell you the silly things that have happened to me in a day; being able to vent and laugh and share. When we finally get to talk, because you're near a phone, the pressure of fitting all the words into so few minutes leaves us either tumbling words over each other or stuttering into awkward silences.

For $5 a minute.

And probably with somebody monitoring the call. It doesn't make the conversation flow really freely, does it?

You have always been my confidant when I need to share secrets, my strength when I'm fragile, and my grounding when I'm flying off on a tangent. Now the world feels unbalanced without you—gravity has surely grown heavier.

I'm so lucky to have found you, and I miss you with all my heart. Worries are too heavy to carry alone. Please come back soon and do something about all this gravity.

**To:** Alesia
**From:** Judd
**Subject:** I miss you, too.

Hi, Sweetheart. We have been flying a lot lately, and I have been wondering how you're doing. Several ships pulled in recently, so the base is chock-full-o-squids and I can never get to a phone.

I'm sorry that you're sad and lonely. I'm just so glad to be able to hear your voice and get e-mail from you. Without those things, it would be unbearable. I do miss you and the children a great deal. You're the last thing I think about when I go to bed, and the first thing I think about when I wake up in the morning.

p.s. Trust me, I miss your cold feet here in the desert.

The loneliness is the worst part. It's impossible to describe. You cover it up with busy days and activities. You get used to being the one who does all the kids' bath times, bed times, and play times. You fill your days with your family, your job, your friends, and the rushing noise of daily life.

But loneliness pounces at night. It lies in wait, knowing you will have to stop to rest at some point. After the kids are tucked in, the e-mails are sent, the laundry is folded, and there is nothing left to do to keep the sadness at bay.

On that first deployment, I tried hard not to let the children see me cry. It was important to me that Connor felt reassured that Mommy was strong, happy, and cheerful all the time.

That's not honest, though. Nobody can be happy all the time, when the person you love more than anything is half a world away—somewhere—and you don't know when you might hear from him. Nobody can be cheerful all the time when facing weeks, months, or even half a year of being apart from your forever-and-ever love.

So, sometimes when Connor cried, I did, too. Just a few tears, enough to let him know that Mommies get sad, too. Enough to let him know that it's OK to miss Daddy so much we cry. Then we talk about how happy we'll be when Judd comes home, and take some kind of affirmative action, like painting a picture for Daddy's box. The boxes were as much for us as for Judd. They helped us feel connected to him, when we hadn't been able to hold his hand, feel his hugs, or lean on his shoulder for so long.

E-mail, wool socks, tears, and boxes. Simple things that helped us count down 183 links in a paper chain.

# Chapter 25

## *Holidays: First Deployment*

**To:** Judd
**From:** Alesia
**Subject:** Happy Dad's Day!

Happy Father's Day! We had cupcakes and sang Happy Daddy's Day to you on a tape that I'll send in your next box. It was fun, but Connor said, "Daddies are s'posed to be with their little boys on Father's Day." I didn't know how to respond. So we went through the whole thing again: where you are, what you're doing, and why you have to be gone. He always acts like he understands, but it's very tough on him. Lauren was just happy to taste the cupcake frosting. From how big her eyes got, I'd say she's going to have her Daddy's sweet tooth!

We love you and are so proud of you for what you're doing. Be safe, and we'll celebrate our real Father's Day the day you come home!

**June 19, 2000**

**To:** Alesia
**From:** Judd
**Subject:** Re: Happy Dad's Day!

Thank you so much for the wonderful Father's Day e-greeting. I really enjoyed it! I've spent the day here in the operations center, working on charts and things for our flights. We have started flying during the day now, and it is a little bit different. It was good to talk to you last night. I miss you all so much, and today even more. I will be flying for Father's Day, but I'll be thinking of all of you.

I'm so proud of Connor for typing his own name! He is such a big boy. I miss him a lot, too. Well, I'm stuck on the base for an hour before the bus comes to take me back to the hotel. We should be moving into the barracks on Monday, depending on the schedule of the Marines who guard the barracks. It's a logistical nightmare and I'm glad I'm not in charge of it. Anyway, I'll talk to you as soon as I can. Happy Father's Day to me!

**E-mail to the Front**

**To:** Judd
**From:** Alesia
**Subject:** Happy Fourth of July!

We went to the parade in town. It was a blast, in the way that only small-town parades can be. Some guys were actually driving down the road in their riding lawn mowers. We really missed you! Happy Independence Day!

**To:** Judd
**From:** Alesia
**Subject:** Happy Halloween!

Connor had fun trick or treating! Malia took him with Kai, since Lauren is sick and I had to stay inside with her. It's really cold here on October 31; very different from trick-or-treating in Pensacola, where the trick was to wear costumes that didn't make them overheat and sweat. Here we have to make sure the kids are warm enough! I took lots of pictures and will send them. I promised Connor that Daddy would dress up next year for Halloween, and we would all go trick-or-treating together.

**November 9, 2000**

**To:** Alesia
**From:** Judd
**Subject:** Happy Birthday to You!

HAPPY BIRTHDAY TO YOU, HAPPY BIRTHDAY TO YOU, HAPPY BIRTHDAY MY DARLING, HAPPY BIRTHDAY TO YOU!!! (Can you hear me singing?!) Hi, Sweetie. I'm sorry I didn't call you last night, but I need to go cash another check to buy a phone card today. Our duty week is finally over. Woo Hoo! Now it will be back to regular old plane washes and reports. I did OK on the 5K run yesterday, and ran faster than last time.

I got another Halloween card from you today, with treats!! Thanks!! I hope you have a wonderful birthday. I'll buy a phone card today and call you this evening so I can sing "Happy Birthday" to you.

I think it will be a short day for me. This weekend celebrates the 35th anniversary of Diego Garcia as a British Indian Ocean Territory, and there is some sort of picnic on the 11th (another free T-shirt, of course). I may go to that. Happy Birthday!

**E-mail to the Front**

**To:** Judd
**From:** Alesia
**Subject:** Happy Thanksgiving!

I hope you got some turkey and pumpkin pie, or the Middle Eastern equivalent (lamb and dates?). We went to a party at Dawn's house with Malia and Kai and had a great time. Wonderful food, company, and conversation. Anyway, the kids had fun and it was great to be among friends on the holiday, since we miss you so much.

I'm sorry you missed Connor's Thanksgiving celebration at preschool. It was really adorable. The kids were dressed up as Pilgrims and Indians and there was a lunch with the apple and pumpkin pies the kids made all by themselves! It was so wonderful, except that you weren't there. Have a safe flight!

November 24, 2000

**To:** Alesia
**From:** Judd
**Subject:** Happy Thanksgiving!!

We had an interesting Thanksgiving; the Omanis did pretty good with the Thanksgiving stuff. We ate real turkey and stuffing with gravy, and also some cranberry sauce. And they made pumpkin, blueberry, and apple pie. It was good, but still a little sad to be away from the family on a holiday.

(Also, there was no football.) How are you and Connor and Lauren doing? I found a video of the over-the-hump party and am going to watch it hoping to catch a glimpse of my beautiful family.

**November 28, 2000**

**To:** Alesia
**From:** Judd
**Subject:** Happy Ramadan

Hello again. Still not much happening here, other than getting ready to come home. We are flying every other day now. Each flight is about 10.5 hours long, so it makes for a pretty long day, but it is good practice for the flight home. Is Connor excited now that there are only a few more links left on the chain? I sure am!

It is Ramadan here, and we had a briefing on the proper protocol. We aren't allowed to eat in public in daylight, for example. I am looking forward to celebrating a second Thanksgiving with you when I get home! Then we'll really have something to be thankful for.

# Chapter 26

## *The Home Stretch*

**To:** Judd
**From:** Alesia
**Subject:** Less than a month to go!!

I can't believe it! This time next month, you'll be home!! When we hit single-digit weeks, it was big, but this is HUGE!! I can't believe it's been five months already. It only feels like five years.

**To:** Alesia
**From:** Judd
**Subject:** Re: Less than a month

I know, I can't believe it, either! Still here at work, getting ready to go to lunch. It has been a pretty boring morning so far. I've been working on gathering the charts that we will need for the trip home. I'll try to call in the morning (your morning). I'll see you soon!

**To:** Judd
**From:** Alesia
**Subject:** I don't want you to feel like a third wheel when you come home.

I can't wait to see you, I can't wait to see you, I can't wait to see you!!!!!

I took the garbage out and thought: Only two more garbage days before Judd comes home!!

I don't want you to feel like a third wheel when you come home, so I've made the following list of "honey-do" jobs for you, in order that you feel essential and wanted:

1. All bath times until June 1st.

2. All grocery shopping.

3. Repair of the following: lawn mower, video camera, printer, digital camera, and toaster (don't ask).

4. Inspection/changing of the following: all smoke detectors, outdoor lights, and you have to show me how to copy a tape from our video camera to a tape on the TV.

5. All night shifts with sick children until June 1st.

6. All veterinary appointments, dog-grooming appointments, dog brushing, etc., until June 1st.

7. Connor's dentist visit.

8. Lauren's one-year checkup and shots in January (I can't stand to see her get stuck with needles).

9. All "I'm BORED, there's NOTHING TO DO" crises until June 1st.

10. All car servicing appointments.

11. Such other tasks as come up and seem only fair to dump on you after the *past* six months.

On June 1st, we can reevaluate and come up with a joint schedule that seems fair to both of us, since by that time I may finally have caught up on some sleep and have some semblance of sanity return.

Be advised: Resistance is futile.

**November 18, 2000**

**To:** Alesia
**From:** Judd
**Subject:** Wow

I'll be happy to do all the things on your list!! The weekend is over, and we are back to the regular old routine here. We just got done with the weekly all officers' meeting. Nothing new to report on when we're coming home, no exact dates, just still between the 4th and the 14th. Our crew will probably be home earlier, since we were among the first to come out here. Since we're flying one of the P-3's home, having an exact date would be kind of useless anyway.

I ran another 5K last night. My time was pretty good, even though I was taking it easy. Got another T-shirt.

I expect that you're giving the kids a bath right now, and getting ready to go to bed in an hour or two. I wish I were there to read some bedtime stories! In a few more weeks, I will be!

**November 25, 2000**

**To:** Judd
**From:** Alesia
**Subject:** Christmas decorations and Jingle Bells

Are not coming out till you get home! I have so much to tell you and can't wait till you get here! Only one more weekend alone after this one! Yahoo!! Love you a lot! Please, please be safe flying and don't let anything happen to you now!

p.s. *You* get to write the Christmas cards out this year.

**November 26, 2000**

**To:** Alesia
**From:** Judd
**Subject:** One more week!

Just a week and then we start flying home! In nine days, I'll be home. I can't wait to see you all and give you big hugs! We're flying tomorrow (finally), and it will be about a 12-hour event. Plenty of fun for everyone. A pretty quiet day here today. I'm going to walk this e-mail over to the Command Center, where the phone line for the e-mail is, and then send it. Then I'm going to take a shower and get some sleep, since we have to be up at 4 a.m. Good night!

**November 30, 2000**

**To:** Judd
**From:** Alesia
**Subject:** Less than a week!

I'm watching the weather channel, and it doesn't look good. If a hurricane delays you, I will be seriously ticked off at Mother Nature. Tomorrow is December, and the month you come home!! Even the *week* you come home!! We have been painting "Welcome Home Daddy" signs like crazy. There are only six more links on the paper chain, so you'd better get home on time, or we're in deep doodoo with Connor.

**November 30, 2000**

**To:** Alesia
**From:** Judd
**Subject:** Weather

I'm getting more and more anxious to see you all. Just a few more days, and we'll be on our way home. The only thing really concerning anyone is the tropical cyclones (hurricanes) that are over the Philippines and the South of India. They may affect the crews from VP-47 flying out from Hawaii to replace us, but we haven't heard anything like that yet. I love you! I have to fly another 10+ hour flight tomorrow, so am getting ready to go to bed and get some rest. See you REALLY SOON!

**December 3, 2000**

**To:** Alesia
**From:** Judd
**Subject:** Hi from Sicily

Hi there! We stopped here in Sigonella, Sicily, to do some repairs and wait for the thunderstorms to quit (also to get gas). We're fine and waiting to see if we are going to continue on to Rhota tonight. If we don't, we will still get home at the same time, as we'll just stop and get gas in Rhota and then fly to Brunswick; overnight in Brunswick and then to Whidbey the next day! Woo Hoo! I'm sitting here catching up with Sean L., he says hello by the way. Gotta run, just wanted to

let you know that I'm OK. Give the kids big hugs
and tell them Daddy's on his way!

The last couple of weeks are an unbelievable whirlwind of activity. Cleaning out his half of the closet (hopefully). Buying groceries
he likes to eat. Painting welcome home signs. You can't believe it's
finally here and are disoriented at the thought of having him come
home. You bite your nails at the slightest hint of anything that will
keep the plane even one day past the due date. One more day, after
such a long time, would be almost unbearable. (And really hard to
explain to the kids!)

But, at last, before you even realize it, the deployment is finally
over. You're dressed up, checking the hotline for any last-minute delays,
and, finally, on your way to the hangar or the dock.

It's Homecoming.

The memories of that first homecoming are still fresh in my
mind. We all looked pretty different at the end of that six months.
Judd had a dark desert tan, and there was a shadow of grim resolve
in his eyes that had never been there before. I'd lost thirty-five
pounds of post-baby weight (the exercise paid off, after all!) and my
hair was a lot longer. Superficial changes, but startling to a husband
who hasn't seen his wife in half a year. Connor had lost some of the
baby look to his face; he was growing from a toddler into a little boy.

The most dramatic change was in Lauren, though. She had been
only a few months old when Judd left and was now in range of her
first birthday. I'd worried quite a bit about how she would react to
Judd. Lauren never liked strangers—especially men. She would
shriek like a banshee when my friends' husbands tried to pick her up
or play with her. I really didn't want her to scream at Judd and make
him feel even more estranged from his daughter than he already did.

Amazingly, through some miracle of baby memory or genetics or just a blessing, Lauren knew Daddy. The moment Judd finally walked off of the plane, Connor went barreling across the tarmac as fast as his sturdy little legs could carry him. No problem there. Then Judd and I somehow met in the middle—I don't even remember walking across. He swept Lauren and me up in a huge hug, and the tears started. (NOTE TO READERS: Judd wants to be sure I point out that *he* just had dust in his eyes. So, the tears were only mine.) Lauren was looking up at Daddy with a huge grin and reaching her chubby arms up for him to take her. Daddy's baby girl knew exactly who he was, even though he was gone for more than half of her life.

It was finally homecoming; our family was together again. It was the best Christmas present ever.

# Part Two:
# Deployment

## November 2001 to June 2002

Time flies when you're having an Inter-Deployment Training Cycle. IDTC is the time span between deployments. For P-3 squadrons, it's one year. The year between December 2000 and December 2001 flew by for us. First, we had all the wonder and joy of reunion and Christmas, combined with the unexpected awkwardness of reorganizing our lives to fit Judd back into them. Then, we moved to a house off the island so I could find a job in Seattle.

After a few months of moving, settling into our new house, meeting the neighbors, finding new preschool and daycare arrangements, my searching for and beginning a new job, and enjoying the beautiful summer in the Pacific Northwest, it was almost time for pre-deployment workups to begin again.

Then came September 11.

I woke up to a phone call from Judd, who was already at work, telling me to turn on the TV. I switched on the news just in time to see the second tower hit. Live. Judd told me to stay home with the kids. He knew I worked on the forty-first floor of an office tower in

Seattle and, like everyone else across the country, wanted to know his family was safe.

Like so many others, I watched CNN all day. I frantically tried to call my family, my in-laws, and my friends. Circuits were down; phone lines were busy. I cried, and I was in shock.

And I knew. I knew that Judd's routine deployment to Japan had just changed. I knew that he and his squadron would be among the first to go deal with the threat, from wherever it originated. I knew military families across America would be gearing up for a long and dangerous mission, just as families in New York, DC, and across the nation were only beginning to realize their grief.

I cried, and I prayed for all of us.

# Chapter 27

## *You Don't Write, You Don't Call . . .*

**December 2001**

**To:** Judd
**From:** Alesia
**Subject:** Where are you and why aren't you writing?

I didn't figure you would have access to e-mail yet there, but am sending this in case you do. I miss you so much, and the kids miss you terribly. Connor has been a crabby monster all weekend. He's very angry and doesn't know how to express it. Lauren just keeps saying, "Where daddy? Daddy all gone?" She wanted to look at the book of pictures of you, from your last deployment, over and over and over today. "Daddy bye bye," she said about the pictures where you are waving to us. I am going to have one or two of those pictures of you enlarged into posters to hang on the walls in their room.

My new baby-sitter came over for a few hours today to meet the kids, and Connor loves her, so that was good. Her name is Bethany, and she's my secretary Jan's daughter. She was a sweetheart with the kids. Lauren even liked her, and Lauren never likes strangers, so I think we have a winner! She's going to pick them up at school tomorrow, so I can go to my writers' group.

I have a killer headache and have to go now. We love you and miss you very much. Write to us!!

---

**To:** Judd
**From:** Alesia
**Subject:** Still no e-mail from you

I took everyone to the Science Center today. It was OK, but we missed you. Lauren was kind of scared of the dinosaurs or "rocks" as she calls them. (Long story, my fault.)

Now we are just kind of hanging out. Nobody feels all that great, except Connor for a change. My Mom has an upset stomach, Lauren has a bad cough/cold and still doesn't want to eat, and I am not over the pneumonia yet.

This is going to be a long and hideous week. I have about 80 hours of work to do by Thursday, then a hearing in Clark County on Friday at 9 a.m. Of course, Clark County is three hours south of Seattle, so that will be fun.

Hope you are well, but beginning to forget what you look like.

---

**To:** Judd
**From:** Alesia
**Subject:** Still no e-mail from putz husband

Am leaving at 4 a.m. tomorrow to fly to Portland for the hearing. I'm exhausted, but OK. I hope you're having a good week, wherever you

are, and whatever you're doing. I had my first
review at the law firm yesterday. It was pretty
good, but I got called "almost pushy" again.

Like the world needs more meek trial lawyers.

Jeff and Doug have been pretty understanding
when I need time off with a sick kid, since you've
been gone. They're both really nice guys with
great senses of humor. (Trust me, this is not all
that common in my field.)

Wish me luck tomorrow and WRITE TO ME!

**To:** Judd
**From:** Alesia
**Subject:** Hello??

How can you just abandon me like this and never
call or write? Don't you care about us?

**To:** Judd
**From:** Alesia
**Subject:** I'm sorry I didn't have much to say when
you called.

It's hard not to get withdrawn when I never
know if or when I might hear from you and have no
way to contact you. Sure, if it were an emergency, I
could track you down. But I don't feel like "I need
to talk to Judd, or my head might explode" is a
legitimate emergency in the grand scheme of things.

You're not the only one with a tough job, even
though yours is more important. I've got a little

bit of stress going on here, too. I do love you, even when I call you a putz. If I didn't love you so much, I wouldn't be afraid you've died when I don't hear from you for days or weeks at a time.

I guess I need to learn to suffer in silence.

**To:** Alesia
**From:** Judd
**Subject:** Re: not saying much

You don't have to say much, I am just happy to hear your voice or know that you are listening. I don't have much to say, either, because every day here is pretty much the same. We are all getting pretty worn out and are ready for a change of location.

You will have to tell me the story about why Lauren calls dinosaurs "rocks"—it sounds like a funny one. I will try to be better about sending you e-mails and trying to call you more often. Sometimes I just give up after flying all day and when the line for the phone is so long.

You should take care of yourself, so you can get over the pneumonia. Just tell me the name of the guy who called you "pushy," and I'll be glad to strafe his office! They're lucky to have you!

I have to go camp out and wait for a phone now, so I can call for Lauren's birthday.

**To:** Judd
**From:** Alesia
**Subject:** Hello darling husband

Sweetie, I know you are not having leisure and bonbons over there, and I know how hard it must be to call or e-mail. I just get frustrated because you are in such a scary place and I worry so much. I miss my best friend/tower of strength/feet warmer. (That would be you, by the way!)
I love you so much.

Judd left on November 30, and it took quite some time for him to contact us. Since we knew where he was and what he was doing, the wait to hear was excruciating. The only way I could vent my anguish and worry was through e-mails I knew he wasn't even receiving yet.

I wish I could explain the feeling of not being able to call and talk to my husband whenever I want. It can be days or weeks of not even knowing what country he's in (or flying over), with no word. It's stressful, frustrating, and lonely. When writing this book, I almost left this chapter out, because I hate the idea that the world may think I'm whiny, needy, and helpless.

I'm not.

I'm actually pretty tough, like every military spouse is. We have to be. But the reality of having no way to contact your spouse for everyday news (there's always a means to track them down in the event of a crisis) is a difficult one to learn to live with. Even after two deployments—a total of a year apart—I'm not sure that I won't start to feel a tiny bit abandoned the next time he has to leave and can't call or write. My head tells me all the smart things:

*He's safe or you would have heard.*

*He's really busy.*

*The phone lines are probably down again.*

But my heart is more fragile, and doubts always aim their poison at the heart, like saboteurs whispering in your ear with their sour breath:

*Maybe something happened, and you just haven't heard yet.*

*Maybe he's in danger.*

*Maybe that e-mail where you vented all over him made him not want to call you ever again.*

Then he calls. Or e-mails. Or flowers arrive, because he's so wonderful he arranged to have flowers delivered every ten days during the entire deployment. And you can fill your lungs again, now that the three-hundred-pound gorilla of fear and worry has been lifted from your chest.

*He's safe. Thank you, God.*

# Chapter 28

## *Six Long Months: Will I Be a Virgin Again?*

**To:** Judd
**From:** Alesia
**Subject:** Abstinence makes the heart grow fonder.

It's been a long three weeks, four days, and 17 hours (but who's counting?)

Here we are, not even a month out, and I am already wondering if six months will qualify me for re-virginization. Can a person die from lack of sex?

**To:** Alesia
**From:** Judd
**Subject:** Think cold showers

**To:** Judd
**From:** Alesia
**Subject:** That's easy for YOU to say!

You're in the desert!

Only four months, 27 days, and 18 hours to go. Maybe I'll take up knitting.

I bet the Joint Chiefs weren't thinking about sex when they decided three- to six-month-long deployments were a good idea. (Of course, once you're one of the Joint Chiefs, maybe you're not allowed to think about sex anymore. Maybe only members of Congress are. It's probably in the Bill of Rights or something.)

Most military spouses don't talk about sex when they discuss deployment. Intimacy is, after all, a very private and personal part of a marriage. But, *come on: Six months is a long time.*

There was a popular movie out recently about some guy who made a bet to go forty days and nights without sex. Forty whole days.

Big deal.

Yet, this is considered so shocking that an actual movie was made about it. With national publicity and hype all over the place— cue suspenseful music—*Can he survive? Will he make it for the entire forty days?*

Give me a break. I'm betting that not a lot of military spouses went to see it. Hollywood, we *scoff* at your forty days.

I have friends who don't mind the occasional fight with their spouses, because of the joys of "make-up sex." Post-deployment reunion sex must be the equivalent of make-up sex times one thousand. In fact, all soldiers and sailors stepping off a plane or boat should have a warning pasted on their uniforms: CAUTION: POST-DEPLOYMENT SEX CAN CAUSE PREGNANCY.

Our squadron had thirty-seven newborn babies nine months after the last deployment. Is there a connection? You decide.

# Chapter 29

## *It's Like Being a Single Parent, But I Can't Date*

**To:** Judd
**From:** Alesia
**Subject:** So, I guess dating is out of the question?

I was so glad you called. I NEVER worry and don't know what you're talking about.

I *was* just kidding about the dating thing. This whole war has really affected your sense of humor. Like I would want to bother with somebody new, after all these years of trying to whip you into shape!

I had a stress-induced baking spree last night and made strawberry muffins, cupcakes, banana nut muffins, and fudge brownies. Everyone at school and work today is very appreciative.

We met seven years ago this month, can you believe it? Seven years, three states, and two children later, and we're still doing great. That's saying something, don't you think?

The kids miss you a lot but are doing fine. They say "God Bless Daddy" in prayers every night and blow kisses to the Daddy posters in their rooms. Nobody is going to forget you, sweetheart. Six months isn't long enough for us to forget you.

Six *years* wouldn't be long enough for that.

# Chapter 30

## *How Will Santa Find Daddy?*

**December 15, 2001**

**To:** Judd
**From:** Alesia
**Subject:** Only 10 days till Christmas!

And we miss you so much! I'm glad we had a "pre-Christmas" with you at Thanksgiving before you left, but it's not the same, since you'll miss Santa Claus. It's Saturday and your son is now a Tiger Belt. He looks very cute in his tiger head-band and special patch with the tiger on it. I keep having to tell him no Tae Kwan Do moves on Lauren, though.

We took P.J. to the groomer's, and now he is clean and smells like a cinnamon-stick dog. They put a festive Christmas scarf and ribbon on him. He seems very humiliated by the whole thing. "Just when I start to smell like a manly dog, they do this to me." I took pity on him, took the ribbon off, and gave him one of his Christmas bones early. He is snoring in front of the fireplace now, dreaming of the doggy equivalent of sugar plums, I guess.

We're leaving soon to pick Mom up at the airport. I hope you can call on Christmas Day.

**December 21**

**To:** Judd
**From:** Alesia
**Subject:** Mommy guilt and Christmas

We went shopping today and my Mom bought too many presents for the kids. She's really into this whole Grandma thing—the kids are thrilled to have her here, of course. I must admit that I went a little overboard, myself, and the kids are going to be VERY lucky and happy little monsters on Christmas Day. I tried to make up for Daddy being gone with my credit card, I'm afraid. Not the wisest course of action, but I was thinking more with my heart today than with my head.

I told Connor that you and your crew flew a mission over the North Pole and saw Santa getting ready. (Be sure to back me up on that when you call.) He was VERY excited and has lots of questions for you about it.

By the way, thanks for the weight bench "you" got me for Christmas. I don't want you to faint or anything, but I put it together all by myself (well, Mom handed me parts) and it actually works. With no parts left over. Pretty amazing!

I will send you a list of what Santa brings the kids, if you promise not to go into some sort of cardiac arrest. They are both getting underwear and Lauren is getting a potty seat, which should please your practical, Grinchy little heart. She went potty on the potty chair at school yesterday!!

**E-mail to the Front**

We had a big celebration, and she told everyone at
the grocery store that she poo-poo'd on the potty.
The teenaged guy who bagged the groceries looked
at her like she was weird, instead of saying something nice, and I said, "It wasn't too long ago
that you were telling people the exact same thing,
Junior."

   Yes, I feel a hundred years old now, thank you
very much.

   (Can you believe it's a year and a half later,
and I'm still e-mailing you halfway around the
world about poop?)

**December 23**

**To:** Judd
**From:** Alesia
**Subject:** So now I'm an elf.

   I just finished a three-hour wrapping extrava-
ganza, so I guess you can figure out that the kids
are getting a little spoiled this Christmas.

   We went to church tonight, and I took everyone
to the movie earlier. *Jimmy Neutron,* boy genius. A
theater full of happy, yelling little kids. My brain
cells melted into my popcorn somewhere between
Jimmy turning his toaster into a rocket ship and
the evil giant space chicken trying to eat Jimmy's
parents. (I was rooting for the space chicken.)

   It's after midnight, and I'm too tired to write
much, but just wanted you to know how much I love
you. This is our first Christmas apart, and I miss

you so much it hurts. I find myself crying at schmaltzy commercials on TV and Christmas carols on the radio. It's ridiculous and out of character for a tough trial lawyer like me.

If I hear "Blue Christmas" one more time, we're going to run out of tissues.

**December 24**

**To:** Alesia
**From:** Judd
**Subject:** Merry Christmas!!!

Merry Christmas Sweetheart!!

I wish I was there to celebrate with you!! You guys are already hip deep in it by now! (Or neck deep, from the sound of your e-mails.) I am getting ready to go flying for 12 hours. Tell Connor and Lauren that we will probably pass Santa and his sleigh.

I'm sure that you are taking plenty of pictures, and I hope that the kids enjoy all of their presents! I miss you all so much. Everyone here is fine, but missing home a little bit more today. We've been really busy the last few days, with not much time for anything else than eating and sleeping, in order to meet our required rest for flying.

Did you see the *Lord of the Rings* movie?? I'm terribly jealous! You know we are supposed to go to all the cool movies together! (I don't mind missing Jimmy Neutron and the Space Chicken.)

**E-mail to the Front**

I love you VERY VERY VERY much. Please give the kids big Christmas hugs and kisses from Daddy, with some extra for Connor, because I know he misses me so much. I will try and call you as soon as I can, but it will be after Christmas your time. Have fun and take lots of pictures!

December 24

**To:** Judd
**From:** Alesia
**Subject:** Sleds in the Desert and Other Tough Questions

OK, my brain hurts. I have been answering tough questions from your son all night long. Here is a sampling:

Q. Where's Daddy?

A. *I don't know where he is right now, sweetie. Remember we looked at the globe and found all the countries where he might be?*

Q. How will Santa find him?

A. *Santa has GPS in his onboard sleigh computer.*

Q. Oh. How will Santa's sleigh get around in the desert?

A. *Well, the reindeer fly him to most places, and he has a team of backup camels.*

Q. What are the camels' names?

A. *I don't know all of them, but I'll bet Daddy can find out for us (beware, this will be coming up the next time you talk to him; I said I knew Omar, Abdul, and Fred were three of them).*

Q. If it's a different day where Daddy is, does Santa really have to fly around for two whole days delivering presents? Doesn't he get tired? He looks kinda old.

A. *Santa rests all year long so that he can make the big Christmas trip. Plus the elves make him lots of coffee for the trip. Also, he's magical, so he never gets really old.*

Q. How does Rudolph's nose light up?

A. *It's bedtime.*

I thought they were never going to go to sleep; they were so excited! We had to leave out cookies and milk for Santa and a bowl of Cheerios plus a bowl of water for the reindeer. Plus a little wrapped bag of cookies for Mrs. Santa. (I drew the line at enough cookies for Santa to take home to all the elves; I said the elves were pretty tired of Christmas cookies by now and were all home resting, watching football, and eating nachos.)

We have been tracking where Santa is on the NORADSANTA.ORG website again. Connor was very excited to see Santa over the Himalayas. It is so cool! They show where Santa is, and some Air Force

**E-mail to the Front**

person gives a "briefing" on the progress. Connor
loves it—he pointed out when Santa was close
to Madagascar and Daddy. (I know you're not in
Madagascar, but that's where lemurs come from,
which Connor thinks is very cool.)

Earlier today, we all went out for a drive,
since it was a beautiful sunny day. Then Connor
and I went out to lunch at Denny's, while Grandma
rested and Lauren napped. Connor ate a whole
plateful of sprinkle pancakes and country potatoes
and told me Denny's makes better potatoes than I
do. I said Denny's just has a better advertising
budget.

The kid doesn't get my jokes.

We talked about how much we miss you, and that
Santa would definitely be able to find you, which
led into the NORAD tracking project at home.

I'd better get to work—I have toys to put
together and gifts to bring out of hiding before I
get some sleep. I have a feeling I know two children who will be up at the crack of dawn tomorrow!!
I miss you so much and will videotape everything
so you can be part of Christmas when you finally
get home. Merry Christmas, my love.

# Chapter 31

## *Fear, Danger, and Terrorism*

January 2002

**To:** Judd
**From:** Alesia
**Subject:** I wish it were a happier New Year.

I read the L.A. *Times* article you sent me about the P-3 manhunt for Al Qaeda leaders. That was more information than you've been able to tell me in a month. Thanks. I forwarded it to our family and friends. I like the logo on your new flight suit patch: "9/11. Terror Cannot Hide. Tracking America's Most Wanted. Operation Enduring Freedom 2001."

It also explains why you're always so tired. Tracking ships for Al Qaeda leaders on the Arabian Sea, one of the most heavily traveled merchant marine lanes in the world, must be a daunting task.

Nobody realizes that the P-3 Orion is one of the oldest planes in the U.S. military. It was funny that they singled out crew members who were younger than the plane to interview. I know some of your planes were built in the '70s. When I hear people complaining about their taxes going for the military budget, I want to scream. The truth is, we need every penny of those budget dollars to meet operational readiness demands. The truth is, if this country wants to have a military ready to go *where* it's needed, *when* it's needed, we have to pay the price. The thought that you might survive missions over Afghanistan and shoulder-fired missiles, but go down due to a broken part on an ancient plane, has crossed my mind a time or two.

I know, I know. You're safe, the planes are fine. The maintenance crew is amazing. But anytime I'm awake at 4 a.m., these are on the list of things I worry about.

**To:** Alesia
**From:** Judd
**Subject:** I'm safe. The planes are fine. Stop worrying.

We are very busy. We had a good flight today. I can't tell you more, but we were all pretty happy. Things are running pretty smoothly, considering everything going on simultaneously.

I know you're worried, but we're doing our job. We trained for this, and we know what we're doing. The planes are in great shape and we're safe. *Quit worrying.* I love you.

**To:** Judd
**From:** Alesia
**Subject:** I *never* worry.

We have very high security at the base. There is a checkpoint to pass with armed guards checking military IDs to get to the commissary. September

11th is still in the forefront of all of our minds; I doubt it will ever fade. The shock and anguish of that day resonated in everyone's hearts.

It has been a pretty subdued New Year's celebration. I think everyone is afraid to wonder what horrors 2002 might bring. We know that Al Qaeda and other terrorist groups have cells in so many different places; lunatics drunk with the grim results of their hideous plotting. Everyone is afraid of what might be next. I admit I was worried that New Year's Eve celebrations would be a big target, especially in DC and New York. I know that there had to be major security and military readiness everyplace like that. But how can you defend against a lone zealot determined to kill people even if—maybe even *especially* if—he has to die to do it?

The 2001 end-of-year holidays muddled by in schizophrenic fashion. Partly joyous at having reason to celebrate after months of anguish. Partly guilty at celebrating, when so many were facing the holidays with an empty place setting at the table, an empty stocking at the chimney, an empty place in their hearts. Partly terrified that death would strike again, in the guise of new attacks by bomb, airplane, or biological warfare.

It was not a holiday season I wanted to spend away from my husband.

But the *reason* he was gone was strong enough to carry me through the loneliness and worry. Our armed forces who were first to respond to the evil of September 11 were all gone for the holidays.

Some on ships that stayed out past the time slated for their return. Some flying missions over and around Afghanistan, like Judd. Some on the ground, searching out the enemy to make sure they couldn't strike again. Here, at home, all military families waited and prayed.

Like I said, it was not a holiday we wanted to spend apart from our spouses. But we were proud of them for serving our country. Standing the line. Protecting the United States. And we prayed that 2002 would bring hope for the future to all of us, so freshly risen from despair.

# Chapter 32

## *On Patriotism*

**To:** Judd
**From:** Alesia
**Subject:** Displaying the flag is cool again.

The questions have stopped.

You remember, the ones I always grumbled to you about?

"Your husband has an engineering degree from Ohio State, why is he wasting his time in the military?"

"Why do you put up with that lifestyle?"

"Couldn't he make a lot more money in the civilian world?"

"Isn't moving around so much too hard on *your* career? Why don't you just stay in one place and he can come visit, if he wants to be in the Navy?"

I don't get any of those questions anymore.

Now, I hear "Thank You." And, "Tell your husband we appreciate what he's doing over there." And, "We're praying for you."

These comments are a lot easier to hear.

I am in awe of the sense of community and pride that has arisen in this country since 9/11. I have always been proud to be an American, but now it's not a politically incorrect position anymore.

## E-mail to the Front

Nobody accuses me of ethnocentrism, when I say this is the best country in the world. Nobody laughs when I cry during the singing of the national anthem.

With Dad in the Air Force, we had some experience with other countries. We were in the Philippines when Ferdinand Marcos decided to impose martial law. Just like that, BAM. An entire country held hostage to his whim.

We were there on what used to be Clark Air Force Base (before the volcano blew), and I was just beginning elementary school, when some of the last of the POWs from the Vietnam War were released. They stopped in the Philippines first, for health care and debriefing, I guess, before heading home.

One of my earliest memories from school is when a very frail, emaciated man came to our classroom. We had a cake for him and posters saying Welcome Home. None of us kids understood what he was coming home *from,* but we were glad to have a party and cake.

Anyway, I was the last one to go outside for recess, and I remember hearing that man talking to my teacher and crying. He was so overwhelmed with joy and gratitude for finally being able to go home. He said the sight of our faces was almost more than he could bear.

I went home that night and told my parents about the man who had cried. I had never seen a grown man cry. My Dad told me that the man had been crying because he loved America so much, and he'd been gone for a very long time. Dad said the man cried because he was so happy to go home.

I see that kind of love for America in faces everywhere today.

Because of the way we grew up, I've known since I was a little girl that there were people who didn't like me just because I'm an American. There were times when we had to have armed guards ride our school bus in Turkey, during anti-U.S. demonstrations. But, like so many others, I never imagined violence reaching across the oceans and into our cities.

Now I know better.

I look around, and I see American flags. They're pasted on car windows and flying from antennas. They're hanging in front of homes and businesses. I wear one on my lapel, like so many others do. When I walk down the halls at work, there are flags on office doors and on cubicle walls.

I've always been proud of you and what you do, even when your being in the Navy means being apart from me and the kids. Now *everyone* is proud of you. Everyone is proud of the Navy, the Marines, the Army, the Air Force, and the Coast Guard. Everyone recognizes that you are heroes patrolling the air, seas, and lands to protect all of us.

And nobody asks me why you're in the military, anymore.

# Chapter 33

## *Enduring Freedom and Enduring Love*

**January 2002**

**To:** Judd
**From:** Alesia
**Subject:** Today I cried at the Ford dealership.

My e-mail to you tonight was going to be about how rough I have it. Work has been drilling spikes in my brain, because I am so swamped. I still am not over the pneumonia I brought home as a souvenir of my business trip to Texas. The kids miss you so much they are entering the monster phase.

To top it all off, I had to wake up even earlier than usual today to hustle the kids to preschool and go get the Explorer inspected, so we can sell it. Trying to sell a car instead of trade it in has been a nightmare; dealing with all the wanna-be buyers and the paperwork issues on my own. The extra $3,000 seems worth it. Some days.

Anyway, this morning I spent a good 10 minutes working myself up to a bout of self-pity as bitter as the dregs of month-old coffee I tried to choke down in the dealership waiting room.

Then somebody turned on the TV.

Today was the day Sgt. Nathan Chapman's family attended his memorial service.

Sgt. 1st Class Nathan Ross Chapman was a 31-

year-old Green Beret, according to KING-5 news. CNN reported that he was the first U.S. soldier killed by enemy fire in Afghanistan. The *Seattle Times* told us that he spent much of his military career based right here out of Fort Lewis, Washington.

I saw him as Renae Chapman's husband and Amanda and Brandon's daddy.

And I cried.

The local news televised the entire memorial service. It was a powerful and moving tribute to the honor, courage, and sacrifice of a man who had served in Panama, Haiti, and Operation Desert Storm, during more than a decade of dedication to his country. But, for me, the story was in what was left unsaid.

Nobody stood up and said "This man vanquished monsters from closets. He played This Little Piggy and gave horsey rides on his back. He changed diapers, gave bottles, and kissed boo-boos. He wrestled and laughed and loved. He gave his wife flowers for no reason and laughed at all of her jokes. Even the bad ones."

But I know he probably did. Because I know you do.

So I sat there in that awful room cramped with orange plastic chairs; the room that smelled of oil, exhaust, and impatience. And I watched and listened and honored this man and his family—all heroes—with my tears.

I was so proud of Mrs. Chapman, this brave woman. I have never met her, and yet I know her.

## E-mail to the Front

She is all of us.

The grace we pray we could attain, if we were ever to open the door to uniformed messengers of death and despair. The anguish we hope never to know. The courage to face an unknown future with fatherless or motherless children.

Every day I wake up to the fact that you could die. That your plane could go down. That some insane zealot could fire a missile and shoot my husband out of the sky. It's never out of mind.

Sure, I put it aside. I have to box up the "Judd may die" thoughts and compartmentalize them out of daily life, or I would never survive it. It is impossible to live in terror and remember to put the trash out. Or bathe the kids. Or cook dinner.

But it never goes away, this fear. It rattles its cage a lot around 4 a.m., when psychopaths and personal demons seem to be strongest. I worry about automatic weapons and shoulder-fired missiles. I worry about anthrax and smallpox and biological terrorism. I remember Somalia, Yemen, and the look in the eyes of those who hate the United States and everything we stand for. So, I pray.

And today I cried.

But, I wasn't alone. The elderly man with the brake problem sat next to me and held my hand. His eyes weren't dry, either. Turns out he spent some time in Korea a few years back. Retired Army.

The harried woman with the red-faced baby and the 30,000-mile tune-up gave me some tissues. Her sister is a helicopter pilot with the Coast Guard.

The service manager stopped to watch and rested a hand on my shoulder. Retired firefighter. His son is carrying on Dad's tradition and his daughter is a police officer. More heroes.

We sat together and we mourned. We mourned the death of Nathan Chapman and the death of this country's innocence. But something beyond sadness and grief was in that room with us. Pride. Hope. Determination.

Pride that we will not stand for the terrorist acts of cowards.

Hope that we will join together in the ashes of tragedy and rise united as Americans.

Determination that our military, composed of warriors like Sgt. Chapman and you and all of the other brave members of our volunteer armed forces, will succeed in keeping our country safe, while protecting the innocents crushed under totalitarian rule.

Grief has tempered into steel in this country in the past few months, borne on the stirring words of great men and women at the scenes of tragedy and in the halls of government.

I felt it happen this morning in a car dealership, through the kindness and strength of ordinary people.

So my message to you tonight is not going to be about how tough I have it. It's about how proud I am of you.

I am proud that you chose to serve your country and its democratic ideals, in an age when many serve only their financial self-interest. I am proud that you are part of our efforts to stand up to those who would gain their ends through oppression, torture, and murder. I am proud that you, your squadron, the Navy, and the combined might of the United States military will teach the insane murderers of September 11th that we will not tolerate their acts of aggression against innocents.

Maybe even as much as all that, I am proud that you love me. I will do my best to be strong and reflect your courage. My litany of woe will become a comedy of misadventure. I promise not even to complain about my ridiculous lack of sleep.

Well, not much.

Please know how lucky I am to have you in my life. The children and I love you and we will always love you. Come home to us safely.

I have a car you might want to buy.

# Chapter 34

## *Back in the Emergency Room*

December 27, 2001

**To:** Judd
**From:** Alesia
**Subject:** Emergency room all night

Your son is desperately sick. He has adenitis, which mimics the symptoms of appendicitis and the lymph nodes in his abdomen are swollen up. He started throwing up yesterday at noon and has kept nothing down since. When he began dry-heaving stomach acid, I took him to the ER. He was so dehydrated they couldn't draw blood. I made them do an abdominal ultrasound and they diagnosed the adenitis. They also did a chest x-ray, and he threw up all through it. We were there for five hours, until 2 a.m., and were pretty much up all night at home. He seems to be holding the ice chips and sips of water down this morning after the anti-nausea suppository (and THAT was fun, let me tell you; he howled bitterly—I wanted to do the same).

And now Lauren is coughing, and I am so worried she will get this, too. I'm so exhausted I want to cry. I am doing yet another load of laundry; after Connor woke up he threw up all over my bed. I gave him a bath and set him up on the couch, and he

**E-mail to the Front**

did it again. All over his clothes, blankets, and pillows. Are we having fun yet?

Perhaps I will just go quietly insane. Thank goodness my Mom is here.

**To:** Connor
**From:** Daddy
**Subject:** Hi, pumpkin

Dear Connor,

Daddy heard that you are sick and that you had to go and see the doctor. I hope the doctor gave you some good medicine to make you feel better. I know that Mommy and Grandma are taking good care of you, and that you will be all better soon. Daddy loves you VERY much. I hope that when you feel better, you will write me another letter, and when I call you will be able to talk to me. Try to take your medicine and get lots of sleep and dream about flying with Daddy in his airplane! I will call and talk to you soon. I love you Connor!!

Much Love, Daddy

**December 28, 2001**

**To:** Judd
**From:** Alesia
**Subject:** Sick Boy

Our sick baby boy had a five-hour nap yesterday afternoon, woke up and started torturing his sister. (As you can tell, he was feeling better!) He still has a cough and had some diarrhea last night, but other than that is just fine. He was hungry and had toast and then spaghetti and slept great and is a bundle of energy this morning! The amazing recuperative powers of kids.

My plans have changed. Now I'll be travelling to Austin, Texas, Wednesday through Friday of next week for work. I'll e-mail you the phone number at the hotel, but it's going to be tough to catch me. I'll have the Blackberry with me, though, so you can e-mail me at my work address those three days.

p.s. No need to be jealous yet; still haven't seen the *Lord of the Rings*. Been a little busy.

**January 5, 2002**

**To:** Judd
**From:** Alesia
**Subject:** Back to the hospital with Connor—
BAD NEWS

Connor screamed when he went to the bathroom this morning. I took him to the hospital and they did a urine culture. Very bad news. White blood

cells way, way up. Red blood cells up, too. He's
got some massive infection. They're starting him
on a strong antibiotic until the results of the
tests that take a couple of days come back. He'll
probably need a renal ultrasound, too.

Evidently UTIs are very rare in young boys—the
doctor said he sees 200 in young girls for every
one in young boys. He was quite concerned. May
also need to do a VCUG, which is a horrible procedure that involves shooting dye and seeing what
happens. It's very painful, and Connor would have
to be sedated.

I am about to go insane worrying about my poor
baby. He has been through so much, and now this??
It doesn't help that I am so sick that the doctor
in Texas who diagnosed my pneumonia wanted me in
the hospital, yet instead it has been nonstop
work/flying/stress for the past two weeks.

I'm going to take my medicine now and try to
take a nap soon. I gave Connor pain medication and
will start his antibiotics as soon as my Mom gets
back from the pharmacy.

Lauren has a cold now too and is cranky, but
refuses to take a nap. To add to the mix, she's
digging at her ear. If she gets an ear infection
now, I am going to take up recreational drinking.

Please pray for us. I am a few inches beyond
the end of my rope. It doesn't escape my attention
that every time I take a business trip, Connor
ends up in the hospital. Can you say MOMMY GUILT???

**January 5, 2002**

**To:** Alesia
**From:** Judd
**Subject:** Re: BAD NEWS

Could this be related to what he had last week?
Poor boy. I'm so glad your Mom is there to help.
You need to make sure that you are getting better,
too. You can't run yourself into the ground, and
then try to take care of the kids, too. I hope
that the antibiotic fixes whatever it is that is
giving Connor problems. I'm sorry that I'm not
there to help. I love you all very, very much.
Please give Connor a big hug and kiss from Daddy.
I love you all.

**January 6, 2002**

**To:** Judd
**From:** Alesia
**Subject:** Cautious optimism

Everyone seems to feel a little better tonight.
Lauren and I had three-hour naps and Mom and
Connor just hung out and rested.
    p.s. My printer sounds like it is dying—why
does this always happen when you're gone?

**To:** Judd
**From:** Alesia
**Subject:** More bad news—Connor

Connor's culture came back with a particularly nasty bug. The doctor wants a renal ultrasound and VCUG. Luckily, one of our expert witnesses is a first-rate pediatric urologist, so I will get Connor in to see Dr. Grady at Children's Hospital and get him taken care of.

I had such a bad headache all day, I feel like my head is going to explode. I've lost about 12 pounds in three weeks—maybe I should write a book. The Deployment Diet: Lose All the Weight You Want Without Even Trying.

I'm very tired of being a single working Mom right about now.

**To:** Alesia
**From:** Judd
**Subject:** Re: bad news

I have been trying and trying to call you, because it seems like weeks since I last talked to you. The phone lines out of here have not been working the last day or so apparently (no one bothers to tell me this when I am sitting redialing the phone for a half hour, of course).

How is Connor feeling now? What exactly is

involved in a VCUG? It sounds pretty awful. We
have been working quite a bit lately, but hopefully will have a rest in a few days. I love you
and miss you all so much! How are you feeling? Are
you getting over the pneumonia? How is your Mom?
I will try and call you again in a day or two (if
the phone lines are up); it's a matter of getting
the timing right so I'm not calling you at 3 in
the morning. But, of course, I am flying whenever
you would be home for me to call. Give everyone
big, mushy kisses from Daddy!

January 10, 2002

**To:** Judd
**From:** Alesia
**Subject:** Connor news/Lauren sick

Last night I talked to Dr. Grady, who is a
wonderful guy. He called me personally because
"it sounded like you needed a little reassurance."
(I guess the gasping sobs gave me away.) He said
we definitely need to do the renal ultrasound and
the VCUG, but it's not urgent because Connor never
had a high fever and is responding so well to the
antibiotics. So we'll do it in the next week or
so. He will sedate Connor for the procedure,
because it's so hideous. A little kiddie Valium to
relax him that also has an amnesic effect, so he
won't remember the procedure afterward. (I asked
Dr. Grady if they had something similar for me,
and he just laughed. I don't think he realized I

was serious; watching someone stick a tube up my
poor baby's peeper is not going to be the high-
light of my day/week/life.)

Lauren has a horrible croupy cough and is home
with Grandma, too, today.

I finally have my voice back and am working
18–19-hour days. It is completely insane. But,
hey, who says I never have any fun—I have to go to
the dentist in about 10 minutes! I love you, but
am starting to forget what you look like.
(Six weeks tomorrow; only 20 more to go.)

Love, your wife (remember me?)

**January 19, 2002**

**To:** Judd
**From:** Alesia
**Subject:** OK, I'm a little tired of you being
gone now.

It's almost 2 a.m. and your poor baby girl has
an ear infection. She woke me up at 11:30 and is
only now going back to sleep. I, of course, being
the selfish awful excuse for a parent that I am,
can only think of how I've only had three hours
of sleep in the past 42. I'm too wound up and
upset now to fall back asleep, because it makes my
heart hurt to see my children in pain and there
has been way, way too much of that going on these
past few weeks.

So I thought I'd vent on you and share some of
my anguish. (Lucky you, right?) Of course, it

would be a lot better if I could come JUMP ON YOUR
HEAD WITH MY BOOTS ON to really express how I
feel. I'm pretty much hating everything about this
deployment. I can't contact you, and we can't talk
when you do manage to call, because the phone
keeps cutting out. Don't ever do this to me again,
or I will go find a nice plumber and move in with
him. He would never travel and, as a bonus, be
useful when the drain clogs. I could learn to live
with the butt-crack thing.

OK, no remote possibility of coherence so will
sign off. I do love you in spite of your current
in-the-doghouse status.

**February 20, 2002**

**To:** Judd
**From:** Alesia
**Subject:** Emergency room all night, the sequel

This time with Lauren. Thank goodness we have
wonderful neighbors. I called poor Lori at 2 a.m.
to find out if I could bring Connor over to sleep
on her couch, so I didn't have to haul him to the
ER, too.

It's 6 a.m. and we're finally home from four
hours at the ER. Why is it that kids always get
sick at 2 a.m. on Saturday nights? I asked the
doctor and she said there is an actual reason—
something about low metabolic rates while sleeping. Whatever. All I know is that they should
label one of the waiting room chairs with my name.

## E-mail to the Front

Lauren woke up and came in my room and said, Mommy, my neck hurts. She was burning up—skin literally on fire—and her temp was 103 degrees. With that fever and her neck hurting, I was terrified that it might be meningitis. So, we went to the ER. They got her right in and the doctor was very concerned. Lauren was lying weak and limp on the table. I felt like my heart stopped beating, and I was hearing words in slow motion.

*Possible meningitis. Spinal tap.*

I really needed you there. I don't even know what country you're in (or flying over). I know I could call Robin and she'd get a message to you but, by then, why bother?

I'm not as strong a person as I thought, when I'm alone in the emergency room with a desperately ill baby. It's just so hard sometimes to carry all the responsibility and worry alone.

They gave Lauren baby Motrin and wanted to watch her for 30 minutes, before going to the extreme measure of a spinal tap. So there we sat, amidst the cold and antiseptic smell, red biohazard syringe box on the wall, monitors everywhere. Lights and beeping. Watching the leisurely pace of the nurses, and then the urgent rush when an ambulance arrived with a car crash victim.

Well, baby Motrin is a Miracle Cure. Lauren was up drinking juice through a straw within about half an hour. Within two hours, she was up and playing peek-a-boo with the nurses. Evidently, it is just some terrible virus. The doctor came back in and said, "Don't these viruses suck?" That's clinical medical terminology that I had to agree with. So they watched and monitored her for a while and then sent us home. The doctor said she should be good as new in a day or two.

I caught sight of myself in the mirror after I took Lauren home and tucked her into bed. I looked like a casualty, myself. I'm surprised I didn't frighten anyone. Lori said to get some rest and call her when we wake up, so I'm taking her up on her gracious offer and going to try to get a nap now. I love you and miss you, but you'd better be here for the next ER visit. It's definitely YOUR SHIFT.

# Chapter 35

## Phone Sex on Monitored Lines

January 2002

**To:** Judd
**From:** Alesia
**Subject:** We are definitely a G-rated couple.

OK, so my idea of saying hot, romantic things on the phone didn't work out all that well. At least we tried. I'm sorry I kept laughing so hard, but the whole situation was pretty hilarious. Nothing personal.

**To:** Judd
**From:** Alesia
**Subject:** WARNING! VERY PERSONAL E-MAIL!

[Editor's Note to Readers: Content censored.]

**To:** Alesia
**From:** Judd
**Subject:** re: WARNING! VERY PERSONAL E-MAIL!

Wow! Thanks for the warning! I'm glad I didn't open your hot e-mail when anyone was around. I miss and love you too, and have lots of hugs saved up for you.

**To:** Judd
**From:** Alesia
**Subject:** Well, THAT was romantic. NOT.

I'm going to go read another romance novel to fill my unrequited needs for hot and steamy.

**To:** Alesia
**From:** Judd
**Subject:** You want romantic, why did you marry an engineer?

Plus, the idea that the phone lines and e-mail may be monitored, and I would be tortured for the rest of my natural life for saying mushy things, is a little inhibiting. Just think, we'll have six months of romantic saved up for when I get home. I am a man of action, more than words.

He had a point. Nothing like the prospect of monitored phone lines to dampen your enthusiasm, unless you're some wacko exhibitionist.

When we had kids, our romantic candlelit dinners transformed into pizza in front of a Disney video, like most people's do. When Judd was gone for six months, my need for romantic, mushy things escalated in direct proportion to the length of time he was gone. So, I came up with the bright idea that we would have a hot, passionate phone call. The problem was, we couldn't really schedule when he was able to call.

In hindsight, it might have been better to try when the kids were asleep. The phone call went something like this:

Me: "I miss you so much. I'd like to run my fingers through your hair and—*Lauren!* Do *not* hit your brother with that hammer!"

Judd: "*What hammer?? Why does Lauren have a hammer??*"

He was definitely getting excited, but this is not what I had in mind.

Me: "It's a toy hammer, honey, from the kids' play tool bench. Relax. Think peaceful, warm, and happy thoughts. Think of hugs and kisses and—*Connor!* Do *not* shoot arrows at the dog!"

Judd: "*Arrows??* What is going *on* there? I leave for a few months, and my kids are juvenile delinquents. With weapons."

Me: "It's his Robin Hood set. Just little foam arrows. But it's the principle of the thing; we don't shoot family members or pets in this house. I'm telling you, you need to relax. You are totally losing the spirit of this romantic interlude we're supposed to be having."

Judd: "OK, I'm sorry. I miss you, too, sweetie, and I —"

Me: "P.J., if you yark on the floor, I am going to sell you for shark bait—*oh, no!! Not on my silk robe!! Why is my silk robe on the floor?? Lauren!!!!*"

Well, even Aphrodite had her off days.

# Chapter 36

## CNN Breaking News Usually Sucks

**To:** Alesia

CNN BREAKING NEWS BULLETIN:

U.S. plane down in Indian Ocean. No details available.

**To:** Judd
**From:** Alesia
**Subject:** Today I thought you died.

For an hour today, I didn't know if your plane had gone down in the ocean.

For an hour, I frantically searched the Internet for further news of who/what/when.

For an hour, I alternated between praying and crying—between hope and despair.

For an hour, I wondered how to tell Connor and Lauren that Daddy was never coming home.

For an hour, I regretted every harsh word we've ever spoken to each other, and wanted to yell at you for leaving me.

For an hour, I wanted to hold you, kiss you, and punch you in the nose for putting me through this.

## E-mail to the Front

For an hour today, I watched my world crumple.
I love you so much, and I'm so glad you're
safe. If you die, I'm going to *kill* you. Don't
ever put me through another hour like this one.

We have the unique privilege these days of being able to see news events live. This is a privilege that, some days, I'd be glad to live without. When you turn on the television or get a breaking news bulletin beamed to your wireless e-mail, you can instantly learn that a plane has gone down, or that a member of the U.S. military has died. But it takes a lot longer to find out *which* plane has gone down. Or *who* has died.

That space in between—the black and terrifying limbo until more details emerge—is the cruelest hurt inflicted on military spouses. First, the feeling like I've been gut-punched. *What plane? I know he was headed for patrols over the Indian Ocean. Is he there now? What plane was it, dammit? Why don't they give us* all *the news instead of doling out these flashes?*

Then, searching the 'net like a madwoman. CNN, the *New York Times,* somebody somewhere has to know what plane it is.

Next, the phone calls begin. All the friends and family who know that he might be out there. That it might be his plane. *Is he OK? Is it Judd's plane? Where's Judd? What's going on? What plane was it?*

As though they believe I have a secret satellite link or psychic connection to the information even CNN doesn't yet know. It gets harder and harder to stay calm on the phone.

A hurried trip to the bathroom. I'm either going to cry or vomit, and I don't want my colleagues to see either. *He might be dead. What would we do without him? What do I tell my kids?* Splash water on my face and go back to the computer to search for any new word.

Then, finally, the knowledge starts to trickle in. CNN breaks some more news. The CO gets a message to his wife, or to the squadron/spouse liaison, and the e-mail chain is activated. It's not Judd's plane. It was another plane. The Search and Rescue team picked the crew up, safe and unharmed. A fervent prayer of thanks for my family and for the families of the crew members who were in that downed plane.

Back to work. Phone calls have to be returned. Documents have to be reviewed. Nobody knows that I just lived through an eternity in the space of an hour.

# Chapter 37

## The Working Military Spouse

**To:** Judd
**From:** Alesia
**Subject:** I'm always the only one in the airport with nobody to meet her.

It's kind of pathetic.

I came down with pneumonia on my business trip, but had a wonderful Texas-style steak dinner. Will tell you all about it when I can breathe and/or talk again.

**To:** Judd
**From:** Alesia
**Subject:** Out to eat again

Only the fifth time in two weeks. By the time I pick up the kids, it's almost 6:30 and they're starved. How do single parents DO this? I am giving Connor the chance to do small tasks that a "big boy" would get to do, so I gave him the money to pay the check. The cashier asked him, "How was your dinner?" Connor said, "Well, it was good, but if I drink too much juice I get diarrhea."

We had the talk about Too Much Information when we got home.

**To:** Alesia
**From:** Judd
**Subject:** Did you have your review yet?

Did they tell you you're wonderful and give you a big raise?

We just got back from flying and I am falling-over tired. I miss you all so much! Don't work too hard.

**To:** Alesia
**From:** Judd
**Subject:** Yes and No

Good thing you married me for my cooking, er . . . my sparkling personality, er . . . WHY did you marry me again? Oh, right. My sense of humor! ☺

**To:** Judd
**From:** Alesia
**Subject:** Working at the Cheese Factory

Connor overheard me talking to somebody about lunch at the Cheesecake Factory, evidently, because he asked me today if I had a good day working at the Cheese Factory.

Actually, the Cheese Factory was a little stressful today. I'd come up with some funny cheese-related metaphors, if I weren't so tired and the thought weren't so . . . cheesy. (Couldn't resist.)

I'm working on that huge project and overseeing other attorneys on it, so I feel an enormous responsibility to make sure it comes off perfectly. Then a colleague of mine (who has no children, of course) said something about a friend of hers who—HORRORS—feeds her kids *frozen waffles* for break-fast! My colleague said, "How hard is it to give them something healthy, like cottage cheese and granola?"

I just looked at her in disbelief, picturing my freezer full of Eggos, and the look on the kids' faces if I were to put a bowl of granola in front of them in the morning. I may as well try to feed them tree bark. All I could say was, "Just wait till *you* have kids, and *then* talk to me. There will be some mornings when you'll think French Toast sticks from Burger King are nutritious enough, if you throw in a banana!"

So, continuing on with my day, halfway through a meeting with a client, I discovered Lauren had drooled cereal on the shoulder of my suit. My client was very impressed, I'm sure.

This is going to sound stupid, but what *you're* doing makes what *I'm* doing seem unimportant, sometimes. I mean, I love my job and work hard for my clients, but "I got a class action lawsuit certified today" seems rather trivial next to "I patrolled the skies looking for Osama." It's a weird feeling. I guess some of us have to keep the economy going here, while you guys take care of us out there. I think a lot of people are feeling that their jobs are less important these days.

**February 2002**

**To:** Judd
**From:** Alesia
**Subject:** Coworkers don't really understand.

I hear "you look tired" a lot. I finally told a couple of the guys that telling a woman she looks tired is as bad as asking how old she is. I know they're just concerned, but I hate hearing that I look as bad as I feel.

**To:** Judd
**From:** Alesia
**Subject:** I adore our housekeeper.

I would rather go without food than give up the cost of having her come in one day a week. When I found myself scrubbing bathrooms at 4:45 a.m., I knew it was time. After I quit the habit of pre-cleaning (so poor Stephanie didn't see how cluttered our house always is!), my life got so much better. (Of course, hers probably got worse!) She is the most organized person I've ever known. I came home one day and the entire pantry was reorganized, with the soups alphabetized and the cans arranged by size. Then, today, all of the kids' books were reorganized in their bookcases by category and size.

I love that in a housekeeper.

**To:** Judd
**From:** Alesia
**Subject:** The "Work" Pie

A lawyer at work actually asked me today if I'd thought about how big the "Work Pie" was going to be in my life as opposed to the "Mommy Pie."

I'm not kidding.

I still have no idea what I said to him. I was, literally, speechless.

Then I arrived at daycare to find out that Connor got in a fight, because he was telling his friends that only girls can be lawyers. I told him that boys can be lawyers, too, but girls are just better at it! (Just kidding; not starting any gender issues in our 4-year-old!)

The "Parent Pie" has to grow considerably when your spouse goes on deployment. There's just nobody else there to cover it. The civilian single parents I know have terrific support networks in place. They often live near family, and have friends they've known forever. But in military life, you rarely if ever live near your family, because you're being shipped all over the country and the world. You make new friends, but it's rare to know someone well enough in a couple of weeks to ask them to keep your kids for a few days, so you can go on a business trip.

You have to find new schools and new daycare arrangements, and then, the *real* fun begins. You have to find a new job. First, you manage to smile through all of the interviews where the first question is, "Why did you move here from *name of state halfway across the country?*" Once you admit the military connection, employers wonder how long you're going to stick around for them. It's rarely an advantage in the job market.

Then, you find a job that may or may not pay anywhere near what you made in the last place you lived. You negotiate the dance of forging new business relationships, and networking from scratch in a new state where everybody else went to college together or has worked together for years. If you have a job that requires licensing, you begin the expensive and difficult process of becoming certified to do whatever you do in this new place.

It's tiring, frustrating, and very stressful. And a little bit of resentment may creep in over the whole process, because your spouse has a job ready to step right into the moment he arrives. Sure, he has to meet new people, but often many of the same men and women he met in flight school or training have been stationed at the same base. So, there are bound to be a few familiar faces, at least. And there's no period of time where he's not earning money, because he's never unemployed.

This can make life a little tense for the unemployed spouse.

Working while Judd was on deployment was like walking a tightrope with snakes and tarantulas underneath it. I never knew what might bite me in the butt if I made the slightest misstep. I used to panic over what would happen if I were in a car accident coming home from work and seriously injured. Nobody would show up at daycare. What if the authorities took my children into protective custody because their horrible, neglectful mother never came to get them? What if my purse burned up in the car fire, so the fire department couldn't find my identification, and I was in a coma for three weeks and nobody knew who I was or how to contact Judd?

Of course, when some semblance of sanity returned or, as Judd said, "I Stopped the Tragedy Train at the Station," I'd remember that everyone had all the emergency numbers. Several friends were on the list to be called if something happened and daycare didn't hear from me. Everyone knew how to contact the squadron if Judd needed to be found.

And I had a system in place with my Mom. If I didn't call her daily, she'd call me. And if she didn't hear from me, she'd call the police. Just in case a meteorite crashed onto my head while I was taking the groceries out of my car, and the children were already in the house, alone.

It could happen.

So, I woke up early, woke the children, made breakfasts and lunches, drove them to school, drove the hour or hour and a half to work, worked all day, made the hideous return commute, cooked dinner (or went out to eat), played games, read stories, did art projects, gave bubble baths, brushed teeth, sang lullabies, watched the news and worried, cleaned the house, did laundry, e-mailed Judd, went back to work on whatever was in my briefcase that day, made lists of what I needed at the store, and, finally, fell into bed for four or five hours, so I could wake up and do it again.

Just another day at the Cheese Factory.

# Chapter 38

## The Great Commissary Shopping Cart Derby

**To:** Alesia
**From:** Judd
**Subject:** Don't forget not to shop on payday.

I got your e-mail about needing to grocery shop. The commissary is always a zoo on payday. You should wait if you can.

**To:** Judd
**From:** Alesia
**Subject:** Oh, sure. NOW you tell me.

There isn't enough Tylenol in the world to make up for this day. I have resorted to searching between the car seats for some—ANY—EVEN ONE—of the aspirin I spilled last week, when I opened the bottle while driving home to the stereo sound of "we don't want to leave the park" hysterics. I feel like a junkie. Next I'll be standing on the street corner with a sign: Will Work for Headache Medicine.

I waited until I had no choice. I really did. Last night I was trying to make a nutritious dinner out of saltine crackers, tofu, and jalapeno peppers, when I finally broke down and admitted that I had to go shopping. After we got home from IHOP—by the way, we eat out way too much. This weekend Connor looked at the dinner I cooked for him and said, "No, thank you, I ordered pizza."

Anyway, after pancakes, potatoes, and much coffee (for me, not the kids), we came home and the kids watched *Veggie Tales* while Mommy wrote out a shopping list. A three-page shopping list.

I was doomed.

So I was prepared for a grueling experience, but I had forgotten the crucial element. The key to the entire commissary experience.

Cue *Twilight Zone* music: Today is Payday.

Not just payday, either. Oh, no. I couldn't possibly just mess up *that* badly! No, today is the first of the month, too. The day when everyone from 19-year-old military spouses to 91-year-old retirees swarm the commissary like a plague of locusts. (Except, locusts are less destructive.)

I finally found a parking space close enough for us to see the building with Connor's binoculars. Then we hiked in to the store, stopping for water halfway when we got dehydrated. We were lucky to snag the last two-seater cart and I strapped the kids in.

Then the real fun began.

I learned today that I'm a total washout at commissary etiquette. I wouldn't be surprised if my military ID card is officially revoked. This total failure at protocol was graciously pointed out to me a mere 497 times by a trio of 200-year-old women.

My first encounter with the enforcers, er, lovely ladies happened quickly. I made the mistake of moving from the bananas to the lettuce and then to the apples. This was, of course, a dire error. "Fruit to fruit. Veggies to veggies," cackled one of the little trolls, er, nice elderly women. "Stay in LINE. Keep it ORDERLY. CLOCKWISE, clockwise!" She was like some produce Drill Sergeant. Connor helped by announcing (loudly, although that goes without saying, doesn't it?), "That lady has blue hair, Mommy."

So I escaped from veggie-ville and made my way to the baking goods aisle. This is where things went from bad to disaster. Fast.

Crotchety old lady #2 was holding court there. With her cart parked diagonally, blocking the aisle in both directions, she weighed the merits of regular Crisco v. butter-flavored for the length of time it took the *Mayflower* to cross the ocean. I finally got a little impatient and gently moved her cart to one side, so we could get by.

As you may know (I didn't), this is a serious breach of cart protocol. You'd have thought I'd clubbed a baby seal right in front of the muffin mix.

"Don't TOUCH my cart! You young people are always in a HURRY!" she screeched. I don't use the word screech lightly. This was a voice that caused sterility in wildlife for miles around. This voice

made nails on a chalkboard sound like Mozart. This
voice . . . OK, you get my point.

We got out of baking goods fast (I didn't
really need to be in *that* aisle anyway, but was
searching for packages of chocolate chips or anything with recipes on it; more recipe cards to
fill out; will explain later) and moved on to
cookies and snacks. The kids were getting tired,
hungry, and crabby by then and doing their imper-
sonations of wild animals who are trying to poke
each other's eyes out. (This is not fun for me.)
I grabbed a box of cookies off the shelf, opened
it up, and gave them each one.

Enter Helpful Lady #3. "You're not supposed to
do that! That's stealing! You haven't PAID for
those COOKIES!"

I tried to ignore her and move past, but she
grabbed hold of the cart and wouldn't let go. I'm
not kidding. I kept saying, "Excuse me, ma'am,
please let go of the cart," and kept walking,
desperately hoping this was all a nightmare, or
at least that she would give up and let go of
the cart.

She didn't. In fact, she tried to grab the
cookie box from Connor! There I was, standing in
the snacks aisle in shock, while a crazed Yoda
clone in support hose and orthopedic shoes tried
to wrestle a box of Nilla Wafers from my son.

All I could think was, "This is Judd's fault."

The tug-of-war lasted about a year (or 30
seconds in real life) and then—you guessed it—the

box ripped and Nilla Wafers went everywhere.
Lauren and Connor both started howling. "Clean
up in Aisle 5" boomed over the loudspeakers. The
women from produce and baking goods had shown up
by now and were shaking their heads disapprovingly.
That was it for me, Baby.

I made it through the rest of the aisles in
eleven minutes flat. (Halfway through frozen
foods, and after the 3,000th "she's touching me,"
I started contemplating how far I could make it
toward Mexico before: a) the kids figured out how
to unbuckle those little seat belts or, b) the
authorities caught up to me.)

Only seven hours, $217, and two or three ulcers
later, we made it home and unpacked the groceries.

I forgot the milk.

# Chapter 39

## Long-Distance Parenting: Just Say No

February 2002

**To:** Judd
**From:** Alesia
**Subject:** Your son is constipated. I hope you're happy.

Just a tip: the next time you tell our son that, if he swallows bubblegum, a giant bubble will come out of his butt and he will be stuck to the toilet seat forever, I am going to hunt you down like a dog. He has been afraid to go to the bathroom for three days.

While we're on the subject, we need to discuss this habit you have of dropping bombs and disappearing. No, I'm not talking about out of your plane. Please observe the following simple telephone Do's and Don'ts:

1. *Don't* tell Lauren that you're on the moon. We had to stand on the porch for 25 minutes last night singing "Twinkle, Twinkle Little Star" and blowing kisses to Daddy, while staring up into space. I still can't move my neck to the left.

2. *Don't* begin any conversation with me about child-rearing with the words, "You really *should* . . ." It's uncanny how you always want to start these helpful little talks when I'm cutting half-eaten Halloween candy out of the dog's fur, or carrying the microwave out to the trash, after Connor wanted to see if heat would speed up the caterpillar-to-butterfly process. Not even Dr. Spock could get my attention at that point.

3. *Do* keep telling the kids that you love them very much and think of them every day.

4. *Don't* tell them that you'll be home "soon." Kids that young have no understanding of time. I had to pull Lauren away from the window, where she was watching for you. She didn't appreciate my explanation that four months is not "soon," if the teeth marks in my arm are any evidence.

5. *Don't* ask Connor how the other guy looked, after a fight at school. I had to explain to his teacher that Daddy did not tell Connor to beat Joey up, exactly. Luckily, Joey's nose turned out not to be broken.

6. *Do* understand and forgive me after I spend a few minutes babbling about how I would have been better off with goldfish.

## E-mail to the Front

As frustrating and exhausting as it can be, to be the parents left alone with the kids, it's important to remember how miserable it must be for the parents who leave. They miss first steps, first teeth, first words, first smiles, and first laughs. They miss bath time, story time, and bedtime. They miss soccer games, baseball games, Chutes and Ladders, and water balloon fights.

Well, OK, let's face it. Nobody misses Chutes and Ladders. Especially after the three-hundredth time. In a week.

So, these lonely Mommies and Daddies try to stay involved by offering insightful opinions on how you should handle any given child-rearing crisis.

From their vantage point of six thousand miles and seventeen time zones away.

Not that it isn't helpful. After all, I've heard such pearls of wisdom as:

- "You really shouldn't give Lauren chocolate right before bedtime," after she climbed on the dog to reach the counter and broke into the Valentine's Day candy, while I was stuck in the bedroom on the stationary phone, because Connor had dropped the cordless phone in the toilet so Grandma could hear the flushing sound. She was up until 3 A.M. on a sugar high. (Lauren, not Grandma.) Of course, that led to:

- "You really shouldn't let Connor play with the cordless phone."

So you give up and just say ummm-hmmm and ah-hah and try not to slam the phone (or your head) against the counter. Repeatedly. You realize that he's just trying to stay connected to the kids he loves and misses so desperately. You work hard to keep his parental presence intact and vivid in the kids' minds. And you realize that shouting, "You don't even know their shoe sizes, don't give *me* parenting advice" is the teensiest bit petty.

Even if it does make you feel better at the time.

# Chapter 40

## *Top Ten Things Not to Say to a Military Spouse*

February 2002

**To:** Judd
**From:** Alesia
**Subject:** You would not believe the things people say to me.

```
    I honestly think they must not think at all
before they open their mouths, or surely they
would never come up with this stuff. If one more
person says, "Oh, has it been six weeks/three
months/[insert time period] already? That sure
went fast, didn't it?" I may wind up on the
evening news for assault. AAARGHHHH!! At first, I
just smiled politely, while gritting my teeth. Now
I give a little laugh and say, "For YOU, maybe!"
```

It's true. Nobody who hasn't been through it really knows what to say. I can understand this. I wouldn't know what to say to someone hit by a meteorite, either. It's just about as foreign a concept as that.

I've compiled a brief conversational guide to help civilians talk to military spouses who are temporarily stressed out of their patriotic minds by deployment.

Here are the top ten things *not* to say to a military spouse (keep in mind that these are all actual statements heard):

10. So he flies P-3s? Those are pretty slow, aren't they? They must make great targets.

9. Well, sure he has to leave for six months at a time, but you *do* get to shop at the commissary.

8. Has it been four months already? Wow, time sure flies.

7. I wish *my* husband would leave for six months.

6. Well, at least you get combat pay while he's gone.

5. Six months?? My husband and I have never been apart more than one night!

4. How do you go that long without sex?

3. (After front-page press on military purchases): So, *that's* where our tax dollars are going??

2. Isn't he back *yet*?

And the number one worst thing to say to a military spouse:

1. You don't seem to be handling this all that well. How hard can it be?

Just for fun, here are a few things we don't want to hear from our *spouses*, either (again, just a few of *actual* statements we've heard):

- Our plane broke down at our refueling stop. Looks like we'll be a few days late getting home from deployment.

- I have to stand duty, so I'll miss our anniversary dinner tomorrow.

**E-mail to the Front**

- We just got called for an upcoming detachment, so you don't get to go on the trip to Chicago with your friend Mary you've had planned for six months. By the way, I'll be in Las Vegas for a week.

- The hurricane is heading directly at us. I'm on the hurricane evacuation crew and will be flying a plane up north to wait out the storm. Please be careful, pack the kids' clothes, and be ready to drive to a safe place if conditions get really bad. I'll see you after the storm passes.

- My leave just got cancelled; so much for our honeymoon to Hawaii next week. Maybe the airlines will understand, and we can use the tickets another time.

- (From deployment): Did I mention I wrote a check for $600 last week? We had enough in the account, right?

- We've got a late flight tomorrow, so I'll miss Connor's birthday party.

- I know you're about to go into labor with our first child any minute, but I have to go on a survival weekend with no cell phones, no radio, and no way to contact me. The duty office said they can send someone to try to find me, if you actually give birth.

- Well, there were no *confirmed* missile attacks on our plane.

# Chapter 41

## *Gifts from Foreign Lands*

**To:** Judd
**From:** Alesia
**Subject:** Thank you for the box of presents.

I'm not quite sure how you managed to tour all of Asia and get lucky enough to find a red velour blanket that weighs 50 pounds and says OHIO STATES UNIVERCITY in 12-inch letters. It's lovely, and I'll think seriously about your idea to redecorate the guest room around it.

The Coach briefcase is wonderful. It's from their little-known subsidiary, SportSCoach, and we passed an enjoyable few minutes at a client luncheon today just reading the tag that came with it. I'm pretty sure you didn't get a chance to see it, so am reproducing it here in full:

HOW TO SERVE THE SPORTSCOACH

1. Dry it in the shadowy place since as it may likey to be deteriolated, if you expose it to direct sunlight or fiire when it is wet by water.

2. When it has scar or stained, to abrade softly by a cotten cloth with wax a little.

3. The products which is damaged in the distribution process or found to be defected in quality will be ripaced with another one, if undamaged.

4. When you wanted to have service on this product please present the warranty for sure.

5. This product is not warranted.

I received several compliments on the briefcase and used it all morning. Unfortunately, it was raining when we came back from lunch, and the shoulder strap melted.

Mom called to say the Japanese kimono is beautiful. She wondered why it says "made in China" on the tag.

The inlaid chopsticks are exquisite. It's handy to have 38 spare sets, in case we have a few unexpected guests.

I didn't realize the neon-green plastic clock shaped like a mosque was actually an alarm clock, until the call to prayer sounded throughout the house at 3 a.m. and sent the dog into cardiac arrest. It only took about 12 minutes to figure out how to turn the alarm off, so the kids and I gathered in the living room to admire it.

We were all awake, anyway.

I really do love your idea of doing the entire house in a carved wooden camel motif, but think we might hold off, since we just bought new furniture last year. Thank you again for the thoughtful and generous gifts. We love you so much and know you are always thinking of us!

The problem with gifts from other lands is that it's so rare that the gift giver has the time or transportation to get very far from the airbase or dock. So the kind of gifts purchased are those sold in the shops that invariably spring up around bases. Or around anyplace likely to be filled with eager buyers flush with a few months' worth of cash in their pockets.

It's just that "Sam's House of Almost Authentic Souvenirs" or "The Drunken Sailor Tattoo, Bait, and Gift Shoppe" aren't likely to have the fine quality of merchandise you might actually want to display in your home.

This is one time when the old adage "It's the thought that counts" definitely rings true. You love him for thinking of you, spending time and money on a gift, and spending more time and money to stand in the long line at the base post office to ship it back to you. You display it proudly, because it's from the person who loves you more than anyone in the world.

And you disable the alarm on the clock.

# Chapter 42

## *Our Heroine Admits She's Not Super Woman*

February 2002

**To:** Judd
**From:** Alesia
**Subject:** 97 loads of laundry later

And your tired baby daughter is finally asleep. Connor is just like his Daddy and falls asleep the second his head hits the pillow. I still have to pack up the stuff to take to daycare tomorrow and finish some work for my job. It's only midnight; what the heck.

I am so tired of being lonely. It makes my stomach hurt. I can't believe we're only through two months—I don't know how I'll survive four more.

**To:** Judd
**From:** Alesia
**Subject:** We have two sick kids.

I don't know why I say "we," but whatever. I just spent two hours in the hospital. Lauren has the baby version of a sinus infection. She has to have antibiotics. So we started the three times a day for ten days pink stuff drill. She has nasty green stuff coming out of her nose and a terrible cough. Connor's cold is getting worse, too. Wahoo.

Since I am living on nerves and caffeine these days, I'm sure I'll get sick any minute. Just added Vitamin C tablets to the shopping list.

**To:** Judd
**From:** Alesia
**Subject:** No sleep again

It's 11:30 and your horrible daughter is still awake. I am exhausted. I hate you being gone. I hate being sick. I hate everything.

Alesia the miserable

p.s. I never thought I'd live to speak the words: "Don't stab your sister in the eye."

**To:** Judd
**From:** Alesia
**Subject:** Mad at you today

OK, first, there is a foot of snow on the ground. The car wouldn't start, because the key would not turn in the ignition. It took me eight tries to get your truck out of the driveway, and I almost wrecked it fishtailing around Everett, because evidently they haven't heard of snowplows here. It took 10 tries to get out of the daycare parking lot.

Lauren is still coughing a little bit, but finally OK to go back to school. P.J. was freaked out by the snow, after three years in Florida, and didn't want to go outside to do his doggy thing.

I had to call roadside assistance to come tow the car to the dealer.

I am sick of being a single mother and having to deal with this sort of thing. That's why I got married in the first place, so I wouldn't have to shovel snow, or worry about cars breaking down or whether the freaking lawn mower starts or not.

I hope you are enjoying Japan.

Here's a secret: You can't always be cheerful. I tried, but sometimes you just get angry. Angry for being alone for so long, angry for having to manage everything by yourself, angry for having no help when everyone is sick at once.

When Mommy gets sick, everything falls apart. And it's really hard not to resent your spouse, the military, and even God, when you've got a 103-degree fever, and you're hanging over the toilet dry-heaving with the flu, while alone in the house with two kids, missing work yet again, afraid you'll get fired.

I read an article once about a military spouse who claimed to be cheerful and happy in any conversations or correspondence with her husband, because she "doesn't want to distract him from his important mission with trivial things at home."

Yeah. Right.

The truth is, it's OK to be angry. The truth is, caring for your children is not a "trivial thing." Sometimes you're so tired, frustrated, and overwhelmed, you almost *have* to get mad and vent a little. Then you get some rest, call a baby-sitter, call some friends, or get help in whatever way you can, and the day brightens. Finally, you feel sane enough to write back and say, "I love and adore you, and I'm sorry I threatened to: set your collection of baseball caps on fire/run off with the towel guy at the health club/sell the children on eBay. It was a tough day, but now I'm better. Thanks for letting me vent."

Most of the time, you can be cheerful and supportive. The times you can't, your spouse will understand. If not, take a deep breath and hang in there. The towel guy probably isn't much of a conversationalist, anyway.

# Chapter 43

## *Top Ten Things a Military Spouse Wants to Hear*

February 2002

**To:** Judd
**From:** Alesia
**Subject:** My personal top 10 list

Here's my fantasy list of what I wish people would say to me to make deployment so much easier:

10. Hey, I can take your kids for an afternoon so you can:

    a) go see a movie that doesn't involve animation or singing farm animals;

    b) treat yourself to a manicure, since nobody else is going to hold your hand for the next six months;

    c) enjoy a little uninterrupted time to yourself for such fun leisure activities as grocery shopping; or

    d) collapse in a heap and try to catch up on a month's worth of sleep deprivation with a three-hour nap.

9. I know life must be a little tough with your spouse gone. If you ever need to vent, let me know. (This must *not* be followed by

unreturned phone calls and unanswered e-mail messages for the next seven weeks.)

8. Whatever that exercise plan is you're doing, it's really working!

7. Tell your spouse we appreciate what he's doing out there.

6. Of course, pizza is one of the four basic food groups.

5. Would you like me to meet you at the airport?

4. We, your bosses, decided you must be tired, and are giving you a month off with pay.

3. Congress just voted a 25 percent pay raise for all military members!

2. We're all praying for your family.

And the Number One, top of the list, absolutely sure-fire thing any military spouse wants to hear:

*Thank you.*

# Chapter 44

## *Over the Hump: Planning a Visit*

**To:** Alesia
**From:** Judd
**Subject:** I did it again

Just when I think I've got the hang of it, I call and it's 4 a.m. your time. Sorry! I'm finally able to check my e-mail today. We didn't even get up to Misawa, we had some problems with the plane after we took off. Of course, one of the reasons we had to leave was that other people were coming in and needed our rooms. After waiting on the plane for 12 hours to see if it could be fixed so we could fly, they finally ended up canceling and putting some of the crew in peoples' rooms that were flying. They sent me to the enlisted barracks for five hours before the maids kicked me out for the next guest. I then spent 17 hours working on projects for the skipper before I had to go find another room to stay in, so I could go flying again last night. Finally, I got my own room last night, after wearing the same flight suit, etc., I intended for an overnight, for three days.

It wasn't the best I've ever smelled.

I tried sending you e-mails to let you know what was going on. You obviously didn't get them.

The base we are on is as big as Everett. In order to get to work, I have to wait for a bus (which runs hourly) or pay for a taxi. To call you collect, I have to use a government phone to call to Fort Lewis in Tacoma to get an outside line. Those phones are all in the hangar, and are usually busy with people running the squadron. I'm buying another phone card to call you now.

I'll talk to you soon. Hopefully, you'll be awake!

**To:** Judd
**From:** Alesia
**Subject:** It's OK—I don't CARE what time it is!!!

I've lost sleep for much less important things than talking to you! We had a wonderful day; played at the park, went for a ride on the ferry, and ran around like wild animals at home playing Fire-Breathing Dragon (me) chases the Princess (Lauren) and the paleontologist (yes, he's YOUR son). Now they're finally in bed, and I'll probably be up till midnight doing the work I need to have done for my job tomorrow. I'm telling you, the idea of being a stay-at-home Mom again sounds pretty darn good on Sunday nights! I could sell Tupperware. I could build a whole Tupperware Empire . . . I could have legions of salespeople . . . no, wait, that's the kind of thinking that always gets me in trouble in the first place.

Everyone thinks I'm nuts for bringing the kids to Japan with me. I don't know why; they're my

kids, they're bound to be adventurous, right? I
love and adore you and miss you—only 24 more paper
chain links till we leave to come see you! And
then you can talk to me at 4 a.m. all you want—in
person!

After spending the first half of deployment flying missions over
and around Afghanistan, Judd's crew moved to Japan. The CO
authorized family visits, so Judd and I decided that the kids and I
would make the trip. We hadn't been allowed to visit during the first
deployment, so we were overjoyed at the chance to spend time with
him in the middle of this one. The logistics and expense were daunting, but we thought it would be worth all of the time and trouble to
get to be together, even for a few short days. We had no choice on
the dates; it had to fall during the week Judd's crew was standing
duty in Misawa, in the north of Japan. Coincidentally, it was the
week before our sixth wedding anniversary.

There were times that week I thought we'd never make it to
our seventh.

# Chapter 45

## Seattle to Tokyo: Two Kids, Three Bags, and Four Hundred Tylenol

**March 2002**

**To:** Judd
**From:** Alesia
**Subject:** Flight attendants are saints.

I found out yesterday that I was the only spouse in the squadron brave enough (or crazy enough) to bring the kids along to see you in Japan for this mid-deployment visit. After 11 hours sealed up in a plane with Connor and Lauren, I can tell you that crazy is definitely the right word. AARGHHHH!!!

We're in the Holiday Inn Tokyo now, and they're finally sleeping. It's only mid-afternoon here, but the middle of the night for us. I needed to take a minute to depressurize (get it? Airplane humor), before I can relax enough to get to sleep.

So, the flight. We had to arrive at the airport two hours early, and I hiked the kids up and down the concourse to burn off some of their energy before they had to be strapped into seats for so long. Lauren developed a new fun way to pass the time, called Run Away from Mommy as Fast and as Far as I Can Go, so Mommy had to run after her lugging Connor and three bags.

## E-mail to the Front

This was great fun. For all the people watching us, at least.

We left her new outfit in the trashcan at SeaTac airport, after she spilled chocolate milk down her shirt and squirted ketchup on her pants. A new land-speed record for clothes staining; purchase to garbage in less than 24 hours. But, there was no way I was carrying food-crusted clothes through two days of travel. They would have walked off the plane in Misawa by themselves. Yuck.

When we finally got on the plane, the real fun began. The family who has followed me on every plane trip for the past 10 years was seated right in front of us. You remember them—Mr. and Mrs. Tiny Brain. The ones with the baby and the two-year old (oddly these kids haven't aged in the past decade).

Yes, in so many years of flying, Mr. and Mrs. Tiny Brain have never figured out that it's a good idea to bring snacks, bottles, games, or toys for their children so they (the kids) and we (all the other passengers) don't lose our minds.

At least this time, they remembered to bring a clean diaper.

*One* clean diaper.

For an 11-hour flight.

So, the poor kids immediately started doing what any small children who are tired/hungry/bored out of their minds/wet/experiencing earache from takeoff do: They howled.

**Seattle to Tokyo: Two Kids, Three Bags, and Four Hundred Tylenol**

And they howled.

And they howled.

The Tiny Brains kept repeating "that's enough" in a never-ending drone, until I wanted to strangle them (the parents, not the kids). Finally, after about three years (or 10 minutes of real time) of this, I couldn't take any more. I handed over some crayons and paper to the older child. I didn't have anything to give the poor baby, though.

At the other end of the neurotic traveler spectrum, I had packed your large leather backpack with enough toys, snacks, and other distractions to last us if we had been traveling to Japan by rowboat.

These held the kids' attention for almost 30 minutes.

Then I was doomed.

I resorted to singing songs (quietly, so my fellow passengers didn't flush me down the air-plane toilet; you know how great my singing is), making up stories, and trying any desperate tactic I could to keep the kids occupied. Somewhere in that horrible blur of time there was a lunch break. The kids didn't eat anything, of course, but had fun unwrapping stuff and poking forks at the various food (??) items.

I have to say, any time my job gets on my nerves, I'm going to remember these poor flight attendants. They have all this special training to keep passengers safe and see to our comfort,

**E-mail to the Front**

yet are treated by so many people as some kind of underpaid servant.

About halfway through the flight, during food service (and what is it with these people whose bladders are magnetically tuned to the frequency of the food and beverage cart?? Any time the flight attendants tried to get down the aisle with the carts, the same people would jump up and demand to get by to the bathroom. Personally, I would have started running them over and keeping score. Sort of a Flight Attendants 500. "Helen rallied on the Seattle-Tokyo leg by taking out the big guy in the Seahawks sweatshirt with the coffee cart, but Jackie pulled ahead by ramming a family of three with the luncheon service.").

That's probably why only FAA-trained professionals are allowed to operate those carts.

Anyway, back to my subject (whatever IT was), during the food service, I asked a flight attendant if she would please bring some milk for Lauren. I said something like, "I know you're very busy, but when you have a free minute after the meal service, would you please bring me some milk for my daughter's bottle?"

She looked at me as if I'd grown a third eye. I was sure I was in major trouble for bothering her, and any minute alarms would go off, and some big, hairy sky marshal was going to come beat me over the head with my tray table.

## Seattle to Tokyo: Two Kids, Three Bags, and Four Hundred Tylenol

But, do you know what she said? In six hours of that very full flight, I was the *first* person to have said "please" to her. Can you believe it??? We chatted a bit during the flight, and you would not believe the horror stories. Just about ordinary passengers and how badly they can act; not even counting the dangers of terrorism flight crews have to deal with now.

Flight attendants everywhere are on my list of heroes this week.

Somehow, we made it through the flight. We ran through every single toy, game, snack, and cassette tape in the bag, plus a couple hundred Tylenol for Mommy, but, out of 11 hours, they were only total monsters for two hours in the middle or so. Thank goodness for somebody's wonderful Grandma who was sitting behind us and played peek-a-boo with Lauren, while I read the constellation book to Connor. (Those Greek and Roman gods were pretty bloodthirsty, let me tell you. I had to edit a lot.)

Anyway, we finally made it. Tomorrow, I have to navigate a bus to the domestic airport and fly to Misawa on Japan Air Lines. I wonder how you say, "Please bring me *sake* for breakfast" in Japanese? I learned one important thing from this trip: I can do *anything*. After changing poopy diapers in an airplane bathroom at 30,000 feet, nothing will ever scare me again.

That trip to Japan will never show up in a guidebook. We saw more of the McDonald's play area at the base commissary/exchange compound than we did Japanese culture. Our one trip to an authentic local restaurant was livened up by Connor calling everything "yucky" and Lauren trying to set her dress on fire in the Hibachi. Not your typical tourist experience.

We did shop at stores in Misawa and at a bazaar of beautiful Japanese art and textiles, though. I'm brushing up on my chess skills to use the inlaid board with the jade pieces without humiliating myself in six moves.

But, unfortunately, I spent most of the week trying to entertain the kids while Judd worked. He had to work 24-hour shifts every other day, so I hung out in the barracks a lot, trying to keep the kids quiet so they wouldn't disturb anybody. Keep in mind that these were jet-lagged kids who didn't understand why they couldn't jump, yell, and dance at 3 a.m.

It wasn't the most fun I've ever had on a trip.

When Judd was off duty—and awake—we experienced such uniquely Japanese events as bowling at the base bowling alley, reading books at the base library, and watching kid-friendly videos we rented from the exchange. We didn't fret about the un-Japanese-ness of it all, though. We just had fun with Lauren's first time bowling, Connor's first orange soda, and Lauren's first snowball fight.

It was exactly what we needed. Time for Connor and Lauren to spend with Daddy, with no pressure of being dragged around on tour buses or on sight-seeing trips that they were too young to understand. Time just to hug and play and remember how much Daddy loved them. Time for Judd and me to talk without a phone line and an ocean between us.

We needed that trip, and we'd do it again in a heartbeat.

When we're all older and wiser (and I've recovered from *this* trip, probably sometime in a decade or so), we'll probably go back to Japan. It's a beautiful country with a fascinating history and culture, and we'd love to see it. But, for just this one trip, the bowling alley was fine.

# Chapter 46

## *Jet Lag and Jelly Beans*

**March 31, 2002**

**To:** Judd
**From:** Alesia
**Subject:** We are finally getting over the jet lag.

It was tough, though. I read somewhere that you need a day for every hour of time difference. No wonder we were so tired! One day shortly after we got home, we slept till four in the afternoon and went to a movie that started at nine at night. The popcorn guys thought I was a bad parent for having my kids out so late; I just know it. But, hey, they're popcorn guys. What do they know?

Your son is trying to comparison count the jelly beans in his Easter basket with Lauren's. I didn't realize this started so young. The Easter Bunny is *not* going to count individual jelly beans to make sure they get the same number. Not ever.

We're watching the Easter video one of the kids got in their baskets, and I'm sneaking out of the room to check e-mail. I hope you got the treats we sent you. Be on the watch for a few dozen hard-boiled colored eggs.

**To:** Judd
**From:** Alesia
**Subject:** Boys lose things and girls find them.

This is unbelievable. You know your thing where you can stand in front of the open refrigerator and not be able to find the milk? How you expect me to know where your car keys, watch, socks, briefcase, etc. etc. etc., are at all times?

It has started already with the kids!!!

Today, Connor was dancing around pestering me, "Where is my other shoe? No, not *that* shoe, the red shoe? Where is it, Mommy?"

I gave my traditional response, "Look for it, Connor. It's not my job to keep track of your stuff."

Just then, Lauren piped up with: "Your shoe is in your closet next to your robot dog, Connor."

Unbelievable. Boys are from the planet Losing Things and girls are from the planet Finding Them. That extra x chromosome must act as some kind of object-tracking GPS unit.

**To:** Judd
**From:** Alesia
**Subject:** Magnetic mind-control devices

Also known as TVs. Did you know that our TV has a mind-control device in it that attracts small boys to inch closer and closer and closer until

their noses are about an inch from the screen? No
matter how many times I say, "Connor, move back,"
he will be an inch from the screen ten minutes
later. I threatened to tie him into his chair to
watch our video, but the kids don't take my
threats very seriously.

I think I'm going to visit my family next
month. Only two more months to go—the paper chain
is getting a lot smaller!

Looking back at the second deployment, it is almost hard to
remember that there were ordinary days. Simple, mundane sorts of
days where nobody was sick, nobody was in the emergency room,
and it wasn't ThreatCon Delta.

But there were, of course. The ordinary days gave us a respite
from the intensity of the rest of it—time to relax and be sane and
recharge our batteries.

Boy, did I need them.

The problem with days when I slept more than three hours out
of twenty-four, however, is that they gave me time to dream up new
ways to torture myself.

Naturally, I decided to write a book.

# Chapter 47

## Flag Waving, Writing, and Other Skills

April 2002

**To:** Judd
**From:** Alesia
**Subject:** I've decided to write a book.

A book about military spouses. I want to call it E-MAIL TO THE FRONT, and use some of our e-mails to describe how crazy this life can be. I want to explain to everyone what it's like to be a military spouse, how we cope, and why we do it. I found a file with all of the e-mails we sent back and forth during your first deployment, and I've been saving the e-mails from this one, too.

I told my friend Pam about the idea over an enormous lunch at the Cheesecake Factory. Pam was so excited she called her agent right then and there to pitch the book to her! Her agent liked the idea and said to send a proposal.

The problem, of course, is that I've never written a book proposal in my life. So I bought a bunch of books on the subject (what else? This is why our household goods weighed over 10,000 pounds; if it weren't for books, it would have been 392 pounds plus the couch) and started writing this weekend. I blasted out a first draft of about five of the chapters.

## E-mail to the Front

It was an unmitigated pile of buffalo dung.

Here's the deal: I want everybody to like me, kind of like Sally Field at the Oscars. So I started "cleaning up" my e-mails. First, I took out all the bad words. Erma Bombeck would never say words like that. Then, I took out all the parts where I sounded lonely, afraid, anguished, or angry. People need to believe I'm strong and tough, right?

Next, I removed anything that sounded like a criticism of deployment or the Navy. This isn't the time to write that six-month deployments seem a bit unreasonable. I need to be supportive of everything the military does. I'm proud of you *and* the military *and* our country; why write anything that detracts from that pride? So I put more flag-waving and red-white-and-blue patriotism in the pages.

Finally, I took out anything that had the remote possibility of being embarrassing to anybody in our family, or to our kids when they learn to read. (I don't want to write a book that adds to the list of what they have to tell the psychiatrist, right?)

After all that cleaning, pressing, spindling, and lemon-scenting, my book had all the appeal of overcooked broccoli. There was nothing left. No honesty, no emotion, no brutal truths. No reason why anyone would read it, let alone laugh, cry, or gain any understanding of the lives of military families.

So (and I guess this finally makes me a *real* writer), I threw it out. All my self-proclaimed pearls of prose, snappy one-liners, and witty exposition. Then I started over. I wrote essays and started pulling the words up from my gut, by way of my heart. I found myself laughing sometimes and crying sometimes, just from typing words on the pages. From rereading e-mails that had seemed desperately serious at the time (remember the lawn mower fiasco? I may *never* live that down), and from rereading e-mails that still cause my breath to hurt, as I force it out of my lungs (the week the USS *Cole* was bombed; the day I thought your plane went down).

What I'm asking you, I guess, is for your permission to share our stories and our lives with total strangers. It's a lot to ask, I know. But I want to help other military spouses know they're not alone. I want to share the lives of military families with those who aren't part of one. It's a story the country needs to hear. Maybe *especially* now.

This feels important to me. It feels like something that matters. Please let me know if you agree. I love you.

**To:** Alesia
**From:** Judd
**Subject:** Re: book

Sounds like a great idea. You're a wonderful writer, and I know it will be terrific. Just keep out all the mushy stuff I wrote.

p.s. When you're a rich writer, I get a classic Mustang.

# Chapter 48

*Family, Friends, and Other Lifelines*

**May 2002**

**To:** Judd
**From:** Alesia
**Subject:** My family puts the "fun" back in dysfunctional.

Here we are at last, after two days of travel, finally back in Barnesville for our family visit. We got in about an hour ago.

I'm ready to go home. Now.

The kids are bouncing off the walls with energy. It's driving Mom insane. They've been cooped up in airplanes and cars for two days and want to run around. She's following behind them, picking up each toy as they set it down. It's like some bizarre circus parade, only louder.

I think Mom's ready for us to leave, too. Now.

p.s. Connor is not a fan of "classic" TV. He was watching *Perry Mason* with Mom, and he said, "You know, Grandma, the shows I watch have color."

**E-mail to the Front**

**To:** Alesia
**From:** Judd
**Subject:** I'm glad you're home.

It makes me worry about all of you less, know-ing you're having a nice visit with your Mom. Say hi to your brothers for me. I know the kids will love having all the Grandmas and relatives to spoil them. Did you see Mary in Columbus?

**To:** Judd
**From:** Alesia
**Subject:** I'm actually delighted to be here for a while.

Even though my family drives me at least as nuts as I probably drive them, it's great to be home for a bit. It will help pass the time in the final month's countdown to your return, because it will only be a few short weeks to homecoming by the time we get back to Seattle. And it's terrific to spend time with my Mom, brothers, and Grandma.

I did see Mary; we spent the night at her place in Columbus before driving out here the next morn-ing. (She says hi.) She's doing really well, and she looked terrific! We took the kids out for mall food for dinner, and let them run around the play area like maniacs and burn off energy from being stuck in the car and planes all day. Mary looked at me at some point during the evening and said, "I admire you for this. It looks really hard, and I don't think I could do it."

I almost burst into tears.

Nobody has ever said that to me—that they admire me for surviving this. I think nobody realizes how tough it is. Compensating for Daddy being gone. Trying to stay afloat at work as a single parent. The constant worry about *where* you are, *how* you are, and *who* might be shooting at you.

I needed to hear it. And I'm not surprised that one of my best friends is the one to have said it. Being apart from you during these two deployments has made me realize how precious friendships are. I know I've told you before how much it hurts to lose a friend. I've been lucky this deployment to have made some great new ones. Family and friends are definitely on my list of blessings.

We'd never make it through deployment without family and friends. My brother, Jerry, always seemed to know exactly when I'd reached the end of my rope, and he'd call from Ohio to listen to me vent or make me laugh. We laughed like fools over Mom and the Great Shopping Cart Rescue Mission, the idea of Velcro playrooms with matching suits for our kids (Time Out takes on a whole new meaning when you can stick them to the wall), and the time the examiner came to question me in relation to Judd's security clearance. The examiner asked me if anybody in my family were involved with any people from hostile foreign nations. I said, "Sir, to my family, West Virginia is a hostile foreign nation."

OK, you probably have to be *in* my family to get that. It's one of those inside jokes that warm you with a feeling of belonging. Like how you know that these people have seen you at your worst—bad temper, neurotic anxieties, and all—and they still love you. That's my definition of family: the ones who love you when you're down and are delighted for you when you're up. The ones you can always go home to, if even for a short while, and know exactly your place in the pattern.

Lots of families have that special closeness. Even when they're scattered throughout different states. I know many spouses actually pack up and go live with their parents during deployment. If they're not working, it makes sense. Three or six months that they can spend with family, letting children really get to know their grandparents. Turning a challenge into an opportunity.

Neighbors can also be a great source of strength. Mine let me bring one child over in the middle of the night so I could take the other to the ER. Lori also listened to my worries and reassured me that I'm not the only parent who ever fantasized about going to the movies one night and not coming home for a month. Or at least until the whiny phase was over.

Military friends understand the difficulties we're facing. Civilian friends offer a haven from having to focus on difficulties so much. My writing friends supported me in my quest to write this book, even when it meant giving up sleep for months.

Each friendship is cherished and becomes part of the network of support we weave around ourselves when our spouses are gone. A few threads at first. We meet a new friend, or feel a special connection to a colleague. She's also a working parent, maybe. Then the fabric strengthens. We find a wonderful baby-sitter; we form relationships through church.

Friends and family are always so high on my list of blessings. Thank you to all of you.

# Chapter 49

## *Our Daughter the Bag Lady*

**To:** Judd
**From:** Alesia
**Subject:** The amazing two-year-old bag lady

I blame Disney for this. Do you remember the pink princess dress I bought Lauren at the Disney store? Sequins and tulle? She has worn it until it's shredded, but still insists on wearing it to school two or three times a week.

I decided way back when Connor was two that letting the kids pick out their own clothes was a good way to let them have control and make choices for themselves. So now I am basically stuck looking like Loser Parent of the Year when we show up at daycare with Lauren wearing this raggedy dress every other day.

Of course, it was a cold winter here, so she had to wear it over her sweatpants and long-sleeved shirt, to be warm enough. She was America's youngest bag lady. The funniest part is that she has that tiny plastic shopping cart she likes to push her dolls around in, so the effect is complete.

Oh, well. As long as you still feel great wearing a princess dress in public, you should do it, right? (And I pretend it's in the laundry. A lot.)

# E-mail to the Front

> **To:** Alesia
> **From:** Judd
> **Subject:** Remember, *you're* the parent.

You should make her wear what *you* want her to wear. She's old enough to learn about appropriate clothing choices.

> **To:** Judd
> **From:** Alesia
> **Subject:** Riiiiight. Fashion tips from Flannel Man.

The day your closet is not filled with varying colors of PLAID, let's talk.

> **To:** Judd
> **From:** Alesia
> **Subject:** Your daughter shows her underwear way too much.

OK, here's an actual note from Lauren's teachers:

"To the parents of Lauren:
If you put Lauren in a dress, please put shorts on underneath. She shows her underwear way too much.
Sorry for the inconvenience.
Thanks. Orange Room Teachers"

(All I can say is, at least she's not in high school.)

When I got done laughing, I tracked down her teachers to get the scoop. I was relieved to hear that Lauren is not doing some kind of baby striptease. She's just like any normal kid that age. She pulls her dress up to wipe juice off her mouth at snacktime, or to wipe paint off her hands after Art Projects. The problem is the boys (it figures!) who start saying "I saw Lauren's under-wear." It's distracting to the class, so now she has to wear pants under all her dresses.

It's not really helping us get past the bag lady image.

# Chapter 50

## *Dear Military Spouse: Official Appreciation*

Every May is National Military Appreciation Month. During that month, one day is set aside as National Military Spouse Appreciation Day. The squadron CO usually takes the time to write a letter to the spouses. Although addressed to "Dear Spouse" instead of personalized, the sentiments the different skippers expressed in the letters were very personal, and I appreciated each of them. With permission of the writers, I'm sharing a few of them here.

12 May 2000

Commanding Officer, Patrol Squadron Forty

Dear Fighting Marlin Spouse,

The Secretary of Defense has declared today as "Military Spouse Appreciation Day." I would like to take a moment to express my sincere appreciation for all of your support. It is a well-known, though rarely expressed, fact that you are an essential part of the Fighting Marlin team. Without your support and commitment, the squadron would be unable to perform as effectively as it does. Your ability to endure the family separations and long working hours required by the Navy enables your spouse to focus on mission-essential tasks and accomplish them to the best of his or her ability.

As the squadron prepared for the upcoming deployment, the work load and stress level increased tremendously. Yet you remained a steadfast supporter of your spouse and the squadron. I also recognize that in the coming months you will make sacrifices that few would ever dare to make.

Although you may be unaware of it, the sacrifices that you make enable the Navy to make a real and significant impact on the rest of the world. It is not uncommon for the work that is done by deployed P-3 squadrons to positively affect the outcome of worldwide events (recent examples include the Persian Gulf War and the Kosovo conflict). Again, your support makes it possible for your spouse to fulfill his or her responsibilities during these extremely important missions nearly every day.

Your dedication and support enabled the Fighting Marlins to achieve unprecedented success during the past year. We won the 7th Fleet Surface Warfare Excellence Award. Our Aviation Maintenance Inspection was one of the best ever conducted by the extremely meticulous inspection team. We had a superb Conventional Weapons Training Program inspection, and a near flawless NATOPS Unit evaluation. Our squadron won the coveted Battle Efficiency Award 1999. Quite simply, we are the best at what we do and we owe a tremendous debt of gratitude to the countless things you do every day to make it possible for us to perform our vital duties.

**E-mail to the Front**

I wrote this letter to ensure that you know that your efforts and sacrifices are truly appreciated. Your support during the home-cycle and the positive effect that it had on the squadron could never be measured. On behalf of the men and women of VP-40, thank you!

Sincerely, Bernie Ryan

May 8, 2002 (posted on the Department of Defense website)

<u>Military Spouse Appreciation Day and National Military Appreciation Month Message From the Chairman</u>

In tribute to the great men and women who have served their country in uniform, May marks National Military Appreciation Month. We are very grateful to our soldiers, sailors, airmen, Marines and Coast Guardsmen for their commitment to preserving freedom and democracy in our Nation and throughout the world.

This year we celebrate Military Spouse Appreciation Day on May 10. As we salute service members past and present, it is only fitting to recognize those who support them and help make their service possible.

Across the country, loved ones have been separated as service members have been mobilized or deployed in support of the global

War on Terrorism. This is a pivotal time in the history of our country and we draw strength by remembering that what is at stake in this conflict makes these sacrifices necessary. Our thoughts and prayers go out to the families that have lost a loved one who gave that last full measure of devotion to their country during this war.

The Joint Chiefs of Staff and I join all Americans in paying tribute to the veterans and current members of our Armed Forces— American heroes past and present—for all they have done and all they continue to do in patriotic service to our country. We also salute our military spouses for their vital, continuing support to our men and women in uniform.

Gen. Richard B. Myers, USAF

11 May 2002

Commanding Officer, Patrol Squadron Forty

Dear Military Spouse,

Since 1984, the Armed Forces of our country have set aside a special day to recognize the countless contributions of Military Spouses. This year, May 11 is designated as Military Spouse Day.

## E-mail to the Front

As Military Spouses, you are often called upon to make innumerable sacrifices as you face the unique challenges of military life. You must cope with deployments, family separations, and frequent moves, all of which require special skills and commitment.

Throughout our Nation's history, Military Spouses have not only met these challenges, but their energy and dedication has helped our Armed Services to thrive. You join a long line of dedicated and loving partners that have enabled military members to serve the United States with honor and courage. Your selfless contributions play a vital role in the stability of our service members, our communities, and our country.

This deployment has posed challenges of communication and Operational Security that many of us have never seen. You have handled these tests with patience, confidence and conviction. I am proud of all of you.

As we celebrate Military Spouse Day, I offer my personal thanks to every "Fighting Marlin" Military Spouse for a "Job Well Done."

Sincerely, D. T. McNamara

# Chapter 51

## *Holidays: Second Deployment*

**December 25, 2001**

**To:** Judd
**From:** Alesia
**Subject:** Merry Christmas!

We miss you so much! The unwrapping was a flurry and the kids are delighted with their presents. I'm a little worried about the Peter Pan Treasure Set bow and foam arrow thing, because Connor has already been eyeing the dog speculatively. Lauren has been walking her new baby around in her baby buggy and her shopping cart all day. We miss you so much, though. Our first Christmas without you, and I'm afraid it probably won't be our last. I taped everything, and everyone said Merry Christmas to Daddy on the tape, so you will eventually see it all and be part of our special day. (Santa went a little nuts here; more on Mommy guilt later!) Merry Christmas, darling. I hope you get a chance to call.

**E-mail to the Front**

January 1, 2002

**To:** Judd
**From:** Alesia
**Subject:** Happy New Year's!

One month down, five to go. Or, 153 links in
paper-chain time. Pretty quiet day here with
everyone sick. I sure hope this isn't an omen of
how the year's going to go. I miss you and hope
you didn't kiss any camels on New Year's Eve!

January 24, 2002

**To:** Judd
**From:** Alesia
**Subject:** Almost princess birthday time

It is hailing here today. HAILING. It has been
cold and rainy all day and now it is hailing!
AARGHHHH!

I had a good day at work, and then took my Mom
to the mall and we did some serious birthday shopping for Lauren. I can't believe she's going to
be TWO! How did that happen? She was just born!
She asked me if "Daddy come home my party?" I told
her you had to work, but we would have another
birthday party for her when you come home. We'll
have one big party for her birthday, our anniversary, your birthday, Connor's birthday, and homecoming all wrapped up in one chocolate frosting
covered bow!

– 226 –

I found a fairy princess costume for Lauren (what else?) with a feather boa, and Grandma discovered a princess plate, bowl, cup, and silverware set that we're giving her from Daddy. We bought Connor a Pooh bear sweatshirt, a Connect 4 game, and a jar of pickles (don't ask), so he won't feel left out.

**January 25, 2002**

**To:** Lauren
**From:** Daddy
**Subject:** Happy Birthday!

Happy birthday, my princess! Daddy misses you so much. Eat a cupcake for Daddy, and then give Mommy a big, yucky, chocolate kiss. Daddy sent Lauren another present. It will come in a box in the mail. I love you, sweetheart. I miss you So Much.
Love, Daddy
p.s. Pickles, Mommy?

**February 14, 2002**

**To:** Judd
**From:** Alesia
**Subject:** Happy Valentine's Day!

I am very lonely today. All the hearts and flowers are getting to me a little bit. I stayed here to work at home today, since the kids' Valentine's parties are at 3 o'clock. That was a big mistake. Being here alone on Valentine's Day was a big mistake. I'm so sad. I know the whole thing is a big marketing conspiracy generated by Hallmark, but it doesn't seem to matter. It hurts so much. I miss you and don't know how I can stand three and a half more months of this. I'm going to stuff this stupid paper chain down the garbage disposal and turn it on high.

I have to sign off and go to the parties now. I'm taking lots of tissues.

March 23, 2002

**To:** Judd
**From:** Alesia
**Subject:** Happy Anniversary!

Can you believe it's been six years of marriage? Six years, two deployments, three states, two kids, and three bar exams. Same dog.

I love you more now than I did the day of our wedding. I wish you were here with me today. But it was wonderful to have our "pre-anniversary" week in Japan with you. The next six years have *got* to be easier, right?

**March 31, 2002**

**To:** Judd
**From:** Alesia
**Subject:** Happy Easter!

We colored eight dozen eggs. I'm not kidding. Chickens across the country worked overtime for this. Connor and Lauren loved their huge baskets; the Easter bunny brought them toys, videos, and little treats and some candy. We had a wonderful day watching our new videos and examining our baskets, but have unfortunately entered the let's-count-our-jelly-beans-to-make-sure-you-don't-have-more-than-I-do phase with Connor. Lauren kept eating hers and throwing his count off.

I told Connor that the Easter Bunny could find you in Japan, so please let him know that you have a basket, too. Would you like 75 hard-boiled eggs in your next box?

**April 9, 2002**

**To:** Judd
**From:** Alesia
**Subject:** Happy Birthday!

Hey, you're pretty old now!! I love your birthday, because for this half of the year, I'm only *three* years older than you! It makes me feel young and, of course, this is all about ME, right? Hee hee!

I hope you got your box of presents. The kids had so much fun making them for you. Be sure to rave about them when you call. I'd sing, but even at this distance, it might hurt your ears. Happy birthday, my love. Be safe.

**May 9, 2002**

**To:** Connor
**From:** Daddy
**Subject:** Happy Birthday!

　Happy birthday, my grown-up 5-year-old boy! Daddy misses you so much. Soon, you'll be in kindergarten! Please write an e-mail to Daddy and tell me what you got for your birthday. I bet you got a lot of cool presents! Daddy loves you, buddy. Only about 25 paper chain links to go!
　Hugs, Daddy

**May 10, 2002**

**To:** Judd
**From:** Alesia
**Subject:** Happy Military Spouse Appreciation Day!

　Only a few short weeks, and I'll be able to appreciate you in person!

**May 12, 2002**

**To:** Alesia
**From:** Judd
**Subject:** Happy Mother's Day!

Happy Mother's Day to the best Mommy in the world! You sure deserve some kind of medal for this past year. Pneumonia, trips to the ER, being on your own, working, taking care of the kids—I know it's a lot. I hope you got my flowers. I'm proud of you, and our children are lucky to have such a wonderful Mommy.

# Chapter 52

## *Homecoming*

June 2002

**To:** Judd
**From:** Alesia
**Subject:** I never thought I'd appreciate the sound of your snoring

But I do!!!

Here you are, finally home (and exhausted), and asleep with both of the kids tucked up against you like puppies, all snoring in unison. They're so happy you're home. *I'm* so happy you're home.

I'm also way too wound up to nap in the middle of the day, so thought I'd send you an e-mail. (What else? E-mail kept me sane for the past six months!)

We stayed all night at Malia's, so we were already on Whidbey Island to come to the hangar this morning. Plus, she kept me from going nuts with the anticipation! I was so nervous. I feel like I've aged 100 years since you left; would you think I looked different? Older? Worse? I had butterflies in my stomach the size of pterodactyls.

As you could tell by the fact he wore the miniature flight suit you sent, Connor's head was about to explode with the excitement. Daddy was *finally* coming home!! I told Clyde and Robin Porter that Connor was probably the only one there with Scooby Doo underwear beneath his flight suit. Clyde said, "Don't be too sure about that!"

Lauren was feeling shy. After all, you were gone a fifth of her life (*this* time). Almost half of her life altogether. But, the minute she saw you step off the plane, she went crazy trying to get down so she could run to you! No worries that anybody forgot Daddy!

When we got home, and Connor showed you the very last link on the paper chain, I found it a little hard to swallow, suddenly. Each one of those links could tell a story. The holidays and birthday parties, the loneliness and sadness, the pancake dinners and pizza/video nights. We counted them down one by one; each link a step toward the day you were home with your family again.

But, in many ways, you were always here with us, my love. Every day, through the hard days and the good ones, through the tears and the laughter. You were the sparkle in Lauren's eyes when she saw her Christmas presents. You were the hugs Connor gave me when we said our prayers, ". . . and God Bless Daddy." You were the strength I needed, when I found out P.J. had a serious heart condition. Your love was part of our lives every day, as though you'd never left. And it always will be, no matter where you have to go, or for how long.

I'm going to sign off now and go watch you sleep. Just because I can. And, tonight, I may even wake you up at 4 a.m. to talk to you.

I owe you one.

**E-mail to the Front**

> **To:** Judd
> **From:** Alesia
> **Subject:** I'm sorry you've been home two weeks and are still living out of your duffel bag.

I keep meaning to find time to clean out your dresser and your half of the closet. I know it's hard readjusting to being home, and having your clothes stuffed into your luggage isn't helping. I promise I will get to it tonight.

You need to realize that we all love you very much, and Lauren is not calling you "my friend Judd" instead of Daddy because she doesn't love you or remember you. She just likes the way your eyes roll back in your head when she does it.

Connor didn't mean to drive you insane by asking you 5,000 questions that began with the word "Why" during dinner last night. That's just his normal dinner conversation. We all thought you overreacted a little bit, but were glad we got the last of the peas scraped off the fireplace before bedtime.

The dog only growled at you twice and, to be fair, you did sit on his chew toy. I'm sure the smell of dog drool will come out of your flight suit after we wash it a couple of times.

Isn't it a good thing we have a protective preschool that doesn't let just any stranger off the street take our children? I admit, calling the police and demanding photo ID was a bit much, but you can never be too safe these days.

The dirty little secret behind reunion is that it's really tough. We build it up in our minds until the reality could never match the anticipation. Then we feel let down when it doesn't.

Not that total joy and happiness doesn't surround homecoming—it does. But sometimes reality intrudes and leaves the reuniting family a little disgruntled. First off, in both reunions we have had, my husband had been up for eighteen hours straight with the rest of his crew, flying their plane home. So his most urgent desire was to go to bed. Alone. And sleep. Not quite the romantic homecoming I had in mind.

Kids who have been counting down the days for 183 links in a paper chain are not inclined to appreciate Mommy or Daddy going off to sleep as soon as they get to the house. So the returning hero is usually tired and a little cranky, in addition to being jet-lagged out of his or her mind. But that's just the first day.

For the next few weeks, we get to play an exciting game called "Let's Push Daddy as Far as Possible Until His Eyes Start Twitching." If Daddy has been gone for several weeks or months, there is no way that children are going to look at him walking back into the house and think "OK, authority figure." It's going to be more like, "OK, who the heck does he think he is? He left us for a long, long, long time, and we don't have to listen to a word he says."

This game is fun for all concerned. Playing instructions are something like this:

Daddy selects any issue and utters a directive to child. Example: "Connor, brush your teeth."

Child has three options, each worth ten points plus possible bonus points:

a) Refuse bluntly: *"No."*

b) Proceed immediately to other parent for counter order. Gain an extra ten points if request is presented in a whining tone that would peel paint off a wall: "Mommmmeeeeeeeee, Daddy said I have to brush my teeeeeeeth. Do I really have toooooooooo?"

c) Ignore directive entirely and stare through offending parent with blank gaze. Gain an extra fifty points if steam actually issues from any parental ear.

To win: Repeat above steps until one or both parents are reduced to whimpering in a corner.

Trying to reincorporate someone into the household routine after half a year takes patience and a sense of humor. It doesn't hurt to lower your standards, either. I have friends who complain that their spouses load the dishwasher the wrong way or buy the wrong brand of toothpaste at the store. Personally, I am so thankful to have somebody else do the grocery shopping, I would cheerfully eat Spam and peanut butter sandwiches for a week.

Finally, keep in mind that the service man or woman who has been gone for weeks or months is used to an entirely different existence, too. For example:

• Out there, they made decisions that may have affected lives. Back home, it's grape jelly or strawberry?

• They lived in a structured environment where everyone responded to instructions with a crisp "Yes, Sir," instead of "You can't make me."

• They survived for several months without seeing a single singing dinosaur or dancing farm animal on television.

Note: Reintroduction to such hyperactive stimulus has been known to cause brain melting.

- They ate in a mess hall, where nobody expected them to wash dishes afterward. Or they worked in a mess hall, so now there's no way they're going to wash another dish for the rest of their lives. Either way, kitchen duty at home will be particularly distasteful.

So it's important to realize that the returning spouse is dealing with his or her own frustrations.

The best advice on how to handle the challenges of reunion and become a family again: Be thankful.

Thankful that he's home to give the kids a bath and read them a story.

Thankful that you can hug or kiss him any time you want.

Thankful that you can talk about your day without paying $5 a minute for a phone call.

Thankful that he came home alive, when some did not.

# Epilogue

It's been five months since our second homecoming. We had the fierce joy of reunion, tempered somewhat in the following weeks by the grief of losing our dog, P.J., to heart disease. It seemed unfair that he'd survived cross-country road trips and cannibalistic coyotes, only to succumb to illness. But, apparently even P.J. counted down the links in the paper chain, because he held on until the week after Judd came home from deployment. Somehow he knew, and he wanted to say good-bye.

These months have brought other joys and sadness, as most months do. Connor started kindergarten, which he loves, and was the narrator in his class play. Judd, Lauren, and I were all there to cheer for him. One of the best days of my entire life, the day I accepted my editor's offer for this book and finally realized my lifelong dream of being a published author, was followed *the very next day* by one of the worst days in my life: the diagnosis of my mother's cancer.

The weeks between then and now have passed in a blur of preoperative tests, writing frenzy, surgery, complications, and Mom's recovery. All of it with the support and love of family and friends. And, thankfully, with my husband home with me.

And all of it under the cloud of a possible new war on the horizon. If we go to war, life may change again. Judd's upcoming "shore tour" may become another deployment to support our war efforts. So many military families will experience again, or for the very first time, the pain, worry, and aching loneliness of separation.

But this is what our armed forces do. They stand the line. And we—all of the military families everywhere—support them, love them, and wait for them.

Thank you for caring about us.